D0579170

# *Betty Crocker's*
# *Easy Slow Cooker* Dinners

Delicious Dinners the Whole Family Will Love

**Hungry Minds**

New York, NY • Cleveland, OH • Indianapolis, IN

Hungry Minds®

Published by
Hungry Minds, Inc.
909 Third Avenue
New York, NY 10022
www.hungryminds.com

Copyright © 2001 General Mills Inc., Minneapolis, MN

All rights reserved. No part of this book may be reproduced or transmitted in any form or by any means, electronic or mechanical, including photocopying, recording, or by an information storage and retrieval system, without permission in writing from the Publisher.

Trademarks: The Hungry Minds logo is a registered trademark of Hungry Minds, Inc. Betty Crocker, Bisquick are registered trademarks of General Mills, Inc. All other trademarks are the property of their respective owners.

For general information on Hungry Minds' products and services please contact our Customer Care Department within the U.S. at 800-762-2974, outside the U.S. at 317-572-3993 or fax 317-572-4002.

For sales inquiries and reseller information, including discounts, premium and bulk quantity sales, and foreign-language translations, please contact our Customer Care Department at 800-434-3422, fax 317-572-4002, or write to Hungry Minds, Inc., Attn: Customer Care Department, 10475 Crosspoint Boulevard, Indianapolis, IN 46256.

**Library of Congress Cataloging-in-Publication Data**
Crocker, Betty.
    Betty Crocker's easy slow cooker dinners.
       p. cm.
   Includes index.
   ISBN 0-7645-6726-8
   1. Electric cookery, Slow. 2. Quick and easy cookery. I. Title.
TX827 .C73 2001
641.884—dc21 2001039154

**GENERAL MILLS, INC.**

**Betty Crocker Kitchens**

Manager, Publishing: Lois L. Tlusty
Recipe Development: Betty Crocker Kitchens Home Economists
Food Stylists: Betty Crocker Kitchens Food Stylists

**Photographic Services**

Photography: Photographic Services Department

**HUNGRY MINDS, INC.**

COVER AND INTERIOR DESIGN BY HOLLY WITTENBERG

For consistent baking results, the Betty Crocker Kitchens recommend Gold Medal Flour.

For more great ideas visit **www.bettycrocker.com**

Manufactured in the United States of America
10 9 8 7 6 5 4 3 2 1

Cover photo: Mexican Pork (page 64)

## Dear Friends,

You've got a new friend in the kitchen—your slow cooker! It cooks all day so you don't have to, and gives you a delicious meal whenever you want. Stuck in traffic on the way home? Putting in some unexpected overtime? Running behind on carpooling? Don't worry, your slow cooker can wait until you get home. And when you walk in the door, dinner is just a few easy minutes away.

Slow cookers offer a super-convenient way to make wholesome dinners for your family. Just pop the ingredients into your slow cooker, turn it on and go about your day—could anything be easier? Many of the recipes here are one-pot meals with little—or nothing—to add to make a complete dinner. Another plus—it's a great way to get finicky eaters to eat their vegetables. After cooking all day, the veggies are tender and succulent, becoming real family pleasers.

Want more reasons to love your slow cookers? There are so many! The prep work for a slow cooker meal is a snap, and for many recipes you can do some of it the night before. Cleanup is a breeze because most of the time there's only one pot to wash. And if your dinner plans include a pot-luck or a casual buffet, a slow cooker is the solution to a no-fuss dish, and it's an easy way to transport your food and keep it warm for serving.

You'll find a variety of recipes—both classics and new favorites—something perfect for every appetite. In fact, once you start making slow-cooker dinners, you won't be able to stop. You'll get hooked on hearty dishes like Beef Stew with Sun-Dried Tomatoes and Italian Spaghetti Sauce. You'll want to try all the fantastic poultry dishes like Chicken Legs with Herbed Onion Sauce and Turkey with Wild Rice, Squash and Cranberries. And there are even meatless options—try Tex-Mex Pinto Beans or Curried Sweet Potato and Lentil Stew.

So plug in your slow cooker for a fast answer to a worry-free dinner that's ready when you are.

*Betty Crocker*

*P.S. Slow-cooked meals are delicious, heartwarming and so easy to make. Enjoy!*

# Contents

# Dinner's Ready!

Are you looking for a simple way to make a delicious, homemade meal, but don't have a lot of time to spend in the kitchen? Then try using a slow cooker! Preparing dinner in a slow cooker is easy—and convenient—because the meal you're making requires little to no attention while it

cooks. Put the ingredients into the slow cooker, then cover and let them simmer while you are working, running errands, doing your favorite volunteer activity or relaxing with family and friends. No matter how you spend your day, a hearty, good-for-you meal will be ready and waiting for you to enjoy.

This slow, steady cooking method fits into every lifestyle. Small families and individuals can enjoy the benefits of slow cooking since you can make enough to enjoy "planned-overs" on another day. And nothing is quite as welcoming as the rich aroma of a home-cooked meal as it wafts through the house. So discover the comfort and ease of slow cooking for yourself.

## Slow Cooker Essentials

### Know Your Slow Cooker

Although using a slow cooker is pretty simple, boning up on the basics is a good idea so you'll be familiar with what your slow cooker offers. Two types of slow cookers are available: the *continuous slow cooker* and the *intermittent slow cooker*. Both are designed to ensure even cooking with an automatic control. They range in size from a 1- to 6-quart capacity. We have included a range of appropriate size cookers at the top of each recipe.

In a *continuous slow cooker*, the food cooks continuously at a very low wattage. The heating coils are in the outer metal shell. The coils become hot and stay on constantly to heat the crockery liner. This type of cooker has two or three fixed settings: low (about 200°), high (about 300°) and in some newer models, auto, which shifts from high to low automatically. The ceramic liner may be fixed or removable. Removable liners offer easy cleanup.

The *intermittent slow cooker* has a heating element in the base on which the cooking container stands. The heat cycles on and off (like an oven) to maintain a constant temperature. The cookers have a dial with numbers or temperatures. Be sure to follow the use-and-care book that comes with the cooker to determine what settings to use. Often, the lowest setting/temperature is only for keeping foods warm, not for cooking.

# Using Your Slow Cooker

### What Temperature Is Best?

Most slow cookers have low and high control settings. At the *low* heat setting, the food temperature remains just below the boiling point. At the *high* heat setting, liquid gently bubbles and cooks approximately twice as fast as on low heat.

It is always best to use the heat setting that a recipe recommends, but sometimes you prefer a shorter cook time. To shorten cook time, use the following as your guide: 1 hour on high is equal to 2 to 2 1/2 hours of cooking on low. So if you don't have 8 to 10 hours for your dinner to cook on the low heat setting, use high instead, and it should be ready to eat in 4 to 5 hours.

### Keep the Lid On!

A slow cooker that's opened doesn't cook, so don't peek! Removing the lid allows heat to escape and adds 15 to 20 minutes to the cooking time each time you peek. Keep the cover on unless a recipe tells you to remove it, and be sure to check for doneness just at the minimum cook time.

### How Full?

For best results, a slow cooker should be between one-half and three-fourths full of food. This helps to ensure that the liquid will not cook away during the long hours of cooking. It also helps keep the food moist and tender.

### Finishing Cook Time

You'll see that some recipes have a "Finishing Cook Time" included. This is necessary when a slow cooker recipe isn't completely "self-sufficient" and a few minutes of additional cooking is required. We've brought this to your attention to let you know that someone will have to be around for those additional 15 to 30 minutes of cooking.

# Tips for Slow Cooker Success

Little tips and tricks often make a recipe come out just right! From a picture-perfect appearance to the fork-tender meat and delicious vegetables, these success tips help ensure each slow-cooked meal comes with a healthy dose of praise.

### Vegetable Smarts

Root vegetables, such as carrots and potatoes, take longer to cook, so cut these vegetables into small pieces or thinly slice them and place in the bottom of the slow cooker for best results.

Thaw frozen vegetables or rinse them with warm water to separate before placing them in the slow cooker. Adding frozen vegetables will lower the internal temperature, and the dish will take longer to cook.

Cut vegetables when you have the time, wrap them separately and refrigerate, then place them in the slow cooker the next morning.

### Cut the Fat

Remove the skin from poultry, and trim excess fat from meats to reduce fat and calories in the finished dish. Skim off excess fat from pot roasts, meaty soups or stews with a slice of bread or with a spoon before serving.

### Seasoning Savvy

Use dried leaf herbs instead of ground because they keep more flavor during the long cooking time. Another way to ensure sufficient flavor is to stir in fresh herbs during the last hour of cooking. Always taste before serving to see whether additional seasoning is needed.

Ground red pepper (cayenne) and red pepper sauce tend to strengthen and become bitter during long slow cooking. Use small amounts and taste during the last hour of cooking and decide whether more seasoning is needed.

### Full of Flavor

Concentrate the flavor of juices in the slow cooker by removing the lid and cooking on the high heat setting during the last 20 to 30 minutes.

Create a more pronounced flavor in soups and stews by substituting broth for the water or adding bouillon cubes with the water.

### Dairy Do's and Don'ts

Dairy products, such as milk, sour cream and cheese, break down during long cooking times, and result in a curdled sauce. Instead of using fresh milk, try canned condensed soups, nonfat dry milk powder or canned evaporated milk for a smooth, creamy sauce. For best results, add cream, sour cream or cheese during the last 30 minutes of cooking time or just before serving to prevent them from breaking down.

## Safety Check

For food-safety reasons, keep this checklist in mind as you use your slow cooker.

- Thaw meat and poultry in the refrigerator or in a microwave oven following the manufacturer's directions. Do not thaw at room temperature.

- Cook and drain all ground meat before adding it to the slow cooker. However, meat should not be browned, refrigerated and added to the slow cooker at a later time. Browned meat is not cooked thoroughly and bacteria can survive. Staph bacteria can continue to grow and will not be killed during cooking, even when the meat is completely cooked thoroughly. Brown meat just before adding to the slow cooker if browning is necessary.

- We recommend not cooking whole poultry, such as chicken, turkey and Rock Cornish hens, in a slow cooker. It takes too long for a safe cooking temperature to reach the bone.

- Always remove leftovers from the slow cooker and refrigerate or freeze them as soon as you are finished eating. Cooked food shouldn't stand at room temperature longer than 1 hour.

- If you want to serve a refrigerated make-ahead dish or leftovers in a slow cooker, that is fine. Just make sure to reheat the food on top of the stove or in the microwave instead of in the slow cooker. Then put it in a preheated slow cooker to keep hot and to serve.

- The temperature in the middle of the food being cooked must reach 140° within 1 1/2 hours and remain at or above 140° for at least 30 minutes at the setting used. For this reason, do not use frozen ingredients, and do not assemble recipes and then refrigerate ahead of time. (But it is okay to cut and measure the ingredients and refrigerate separately ahead of time. Just don't combine them until you are ready to cook.) Refrigerated ingredients, such as meat and poultry, can be used right from the refrigerator.

- Don't undercook foods. Check the internal temperature with an instant read thermometer to be sure that poultry has reached 170° and large cuts of meat have reached 155°.

## High Altitude Tips

For people who live at higher altitudes (3,500 feet and above), everyday cooking has some challenges, and slow cooking is no exception. Unfortunately, trial and error often is the only way to make improvements because no set rules apply to all recipes.

Here are some guidelines to keep in mind when using your cooker:

Most foods will take longer to cook, particularly meats cooked in boiling liquid. Sometimes it takes twice as long than the recipe suggests for meats to become tender. You might want to try cooking meats on high heat setting rather than low to help shorten the cooking time.

Dried beans also will cook more slowly. We recommend using the method of soaking them overnight in water before cooking in the slow cooker.

Call your local U.S. Department of Agriculture (USDA) Extension Service office, listed in the phone book under county government, with questions about slow cooking at high altitude.

# Chapter 1

# Hearty Beef and Pork Main Dishes

Photos, clockwise from top left: Easy French Dip Sandwiches (page 24), Mediterranean Pot Roast (page 10), Roast Pork with Fruit (page 18), Pork and Potatoes with Rosemary (page 20)

# Mediterranean Pot Roast

**Slow Cooker** 4- to 5-quart • **Prep Time** 10 min • **Cook Time** Low 5 to 6 hr • **Stand** 15 min

3-pound beef boneless chuck roast

1 teaspoon salt

1 tablespoon dried Italian seasoning

1 large clove garlic, finely chopped

1/3 cup oil-packed sun-dried
   tomatoes, drained and chopped

1/2 cup sliced pitted Kalamata or
   ripe olives

1/2 cup beef broth

1/2 cup frozen pearl onions
   (from 16-ounce bag)

*1.* Spray 12-inch skillet with cooking spray; heat over medium-high heat. Cook beef in skillet about 5 minutes, turning once, until brown. Sprinkle with salt, Italian seasoning and garlic; remove from skillet.

*2.* Place beef, seasoned side up, in 4- to 5-quart slow cooker. Spread tomatoes and olives over roast. Add broth and onions.

*3.* Cover and cook on low heat setting 5 to 6 hours or until beef is tender.

*4.* Remove beef from slow cooker; cover and let stand 15 minutes. Slice beef; serve with beef juice and onions from slow cooker.

**1 Serving:**
Calories 220 (Calories from Fat 115);
Fat 13g (Saturated 5g); Cholesterol 60mg;
Sodium 470mg; Carbohydrate 5g
(Dietary Fiber 1g); Protein 22g

**% Daily Value:**
Vitamin A 0%; Vitamin C 4%; Calcium 2%;
Iron 16%

**Diet Exchanges:**
3 Lean Meat, 1 Vegetable, 1/2 Fat

*Serving Suggestion* Fluffy homemade mashed potatoes are the perfect partner for beef roast. Leave the skins on or off—it's up to you.

Mediterranean Pot Roast

# Savory Pot Roast

**Slow Cooker** 4- to 6-quart • **Prep Time** 20 min • **Cook Time** Low 8 to 10 hr • **Finishing Cook Time** High 15 min

2- to 2 1/2-pound beef bottom round roast

2 teaspoons olive or vegetable oil

2 or 3 medium potatoes, cut into 2-inch pieces

2 1/2 cups baby-cut carrots

2 cups sliced mushrooms (about 5 ounces)

1 medium stalk celery, sliced (1/2 cup)

1 medium onion, chopped (1/2 cup)

1 teaspoon salt

1/2 teaspoon pepper

1/2 teaspoon dried thyme leaves

1 can (14 1/2 ounces) diced tomatoes, undrained

1 can (10 1/2 ounces) condensed beef broth

1 can (5 1/2 ounces) eight-vegetable juice

1/4 cup all-purpose flour

*1.* Trim excess fat from beef. Heat oil in 10-inch skillet over medium-high heat. Cook beef in oil about 10 minutes, turning occasionally, until brown on all sides.

*2.* Place potatoes, carrots, mushrooms, celery and onion in 4- to 6-quart slow cooker. Sprinkle with salt, pepper and thyme. Place beef on vegetables. Pour tomatoes, broth and vegetable juice over beef.

*3.* Cover and cook on low heat setting 8 to 10 hours or until beef and vegetables are tender.

*4.* Remove beef and vegetables from cooker, using slotted spoon; place on serving platter and keep warm.

*5.* Skim fat from beef juices in cooker if desired. Remove 1/2 cup of the juices from the cooker; mix with flour until smooth. Gradually stir flour mixture into remaining juices in cooker. Cook on high heat setting about 15 minutes or until thickened. Serve sauce with beef and vegetables.

*Betty's Success Tip*    A quick way to mix the flour with the liquid is to use a jar. Screw the lid on tight, and shake the jar until the mixture is smooth. This is faster than trying to stir it until all the lumps of flour are dissolved.

*Ingredient Substitution*    If you only have tomato juice in your cupboard, go ahead and use it instead of the eight-vegetable juice. Regular-size carrots, cut into 2-inch pieces, can be used if you are out of baby-cut carrots. And a drained 4-ounce can of sliced mushrooms can be used instead of the fresh mushrooms.

**1 Serving:**
Calories 270 (Calories from Fat 55);
Fat 6g (Saturated 2g); Cholesterol 75mg;
Sodium 880mg; Carbohydrate 26g
(Dietary Fiber 4g); Protein 32g

**% Daily Value:**
Vitamin A 90%; Vitamin C 24%; Calcium 6%;
Iron 26%

**Diet Exchanges:**
1 Starch, 3 Lean Meat, 2 Vegetable

Savory Pot Roast

# Brisket with Cranberry Gravy

**Slow Cooker** 4- to 6-quart • **Prep Time** 10 min • **Cook Time** Low 8 to 10 hr

2 1/2-pound fresh beef brisket (not corned beef)

1/2 teaspoon salt

1/4 teaspoon pepper

1 can (16 ounces) whole berry cranberry sauce

1 can (8 ounces) tomato sauce

1 medium onion, chopped (1/2 cup)

1 tablespoon mustard

*1.* Trim excess fat from beef. Rub surface of beef with salt and pepper. Place beef in 4- to 6-quart slow cooker. Mix remaining ingredients; pour over beef.

*2.* Cover and cook on low heat setting 8 to 10 hours or until beef is tender.

*3.* Cut beef across grain into thin slices. Skim fat from cranberry sauce in cooker if desired; serve with beef.

---

*Betty's Success Tip*   Be sure to use a fresh beef brisket instead of a corned beef brisket. A "corned" brisket is a fresh brisket that has been cured in seasoned brine, which would overpower the delicate flavor of the cranberry gravy. If a fresh brisket isn't available, use the same cut of beef roast that you use for your favorite pot roast.

*Ingredient Substitution*   We like the appearance of the whole berry cranberry sauce, but you can use a can of jellied cranberries if you like.

**1 Serving:**
Calories 265 (Calories from Fat 70); Fat 8g (Saturated 3g); Cholesterol 60mg; Sodium 410mg; Carbohydrate 25g (Dietary Fiber 1g); Protein 24g

**% Daily Value:**
Vitamin A 2%; Vitamin C 4%; Calcium 2%; Iron 12%

**Diet Exchanges:**
1 Starch, 2 1/2 Lean Meat, 2 Vegetable

# Swiss Steak

**6 servings**

**Slow Cooker** 3 1/2- to 6-quart • **Prep Time** 15 min • **Cook Time** Low 7 to 9 hr

3 tablespoons all-purpose flour

1 teaspoon ground mustard

1/2 teaspoon salt

1 1/2 pound beef boneless round, tip or chuck steak, about 3/4 inch thick, cut into 6 pieces

2 tablespoons vegetable oil

1 large onion, sliced

1 large bell pepper, sliced

1 can (14 1/2 ounces) diced tomatoes, undrained

2 cloves garlic, finely chopped

*1.* Mix flour, mustard and salt. Coat beef with flour mixture.

*2.* Heat oil in 10-inch skillet over medium heat. Cook beef in oil about 15 minutes, turning once, until brown.

*3.* Place beef in 3 1/2- to 6-quart slow cooker; top with onion and bell pepper. Mix tomatoes and garlic; pour over beef and vegetables. Cover and cook on low heat setting 7 to 9 hours or until beef is tender.

**1 Serving:**
Calories 190 (Calories from Fat 65); Fat 7g (Saturated 2g); Cholesterol 60mg; Sodium 340mg; Carbohydrate 10g (Dietary Fiber 2g); Protein 24g

**% Daily Value:**
Vitamin A 6%; Vitamin C 30%; Calcium 2%; Iron 16%

**Diet Exchanges:**
3 Lean Meat, 2 Vegetable

*Betty's Success Tip*   If you like, remove any excess fat from the beef before browning in the skillet.

*Ingredient Substitution*   Use 1 can (14 1/2 ounces) of diced tomatoes with garlic, and omit the garlic cloves.

# Beef Stroganoff

**Slow Cooker** 3 1/2- to 6-quart • **Prep Time** 10 min • **Cook Time** Low 8 to 10 hr

2 pounds beef stew meat

1 large onion, chopped (1 cup)

1 can (10 3/4 ounces) condensed
cream of golden mushroom soup

1 can (10 3/4 ounces) condensed
cream of onion soup

1 can (8 ounces) sliced mushrooms,
drained

1/4 teaspoon pepper

1 package (8 ounces) cream cheese,
cubed

1 container (8 ounces) sour cream

6 cups hot cooked noodles or rice,
for serving, if desired

*1.* Mix beef, onion, soups, mushrooms and pepper in 3 1/2- to
6-quart slow cooker.

*2.* Cover and cook on low heat setting 8 to 10 hours or until beef is
very tender.

*3.* Stir cream cheese into beef mixture until melted. Stir in sour cream.

*4.* Serve beef mixture over noodles.

*Betty's Success Tip*   The soups not only add flavor but also provide
a smooth and creamy sauce for this stroganoff. The sour cream is
stirred in at the end of cooking so it stays smooth and doesn't curdle
the sauce.

*Finishing Touch*   Make this stroganoff extra special by replacing the
canned mushrooms with sliced fresh mushrooms you add at the end of
cooking. Sauté the mushrooms in a small amount of butter just until
they brown. Stir mushrooms in with the sour cream. Top off the
stroganoff with a generous sprinkle of freshly chopped parsley.

**1 Serving:**
Calories 505 (Calories from Fat 325);
Fat 36g (Saturated 17g); Cholesterol 145mg;
Sodium 830mg; Carbohydrate 12g
(Dietary Fiber 1g); Protein 34g

**% Daily Value:**
Vitamin A 14%; Vitamin C 2%; Calcium 12%;
Iron 22%

**Diet Exchanges:**
4 High-Fat Meat, 2 Vegetable, 1 Fat

# Cheesy Italian Tortellini

**Slow Cooker** 4- to 5-quart • **Prep Time** 15 min • **Cook Time** Low 7 to 8 hr • **Finishing Cook Time** Low 15 min

1/2 pound ground beef

1/2 pound Italian sausage

1 container (15 ounces) refrigerated marinara sauce

1 cup sliced fresh mushrooms

1 can (14 1/2 ounces) diced tomatoes with Italian seasonings, undrained

1 package (9 ounces) refrigerated cheese tortellini

1 cup shredded mozzarella or pizza-style cheese (4 ounces)

*1.* Break beef and sausage into large pieces in 10-inch skillet. Cook over medium heat about 10 minutes, stirring occasionally, or until brown.

*2.* Mix beef mixture, marinara sauce, mushrooms and tomatoes in slow cooker.

*3.* Cover and cook on low heat setting 7 to 8 hours. Stir in tortellini; sprinkle with cheese. Cover and cook on low heat setting about 15 minutes longer or until tortellini is tender.

**1 Serving:**
Calories 550 (Calories from Fat 280);
Fat 31g (Saturated 12g); Cholesterol 135mg;
Sodium 1260mg; Carbohydrate 37g
(Dietary Fiber 3g); Protein 34g

**% Daily Value:**
Vitamin A 22%; Vitamin C 26%; Calcium 32%;
Iron 22%

**Diet Exchanges:**
2 Starch, 4 Medium-Fat Meat, 1 Vegetable,
1 1/2 Fat

*Ingredient Substitution*  A can of plain diced tomatoes and 1/2 teaspoon dried Italian seasoning can be used instead of the diced tomatoes with Italian seasoning.

# Roast Pork with Fruit

**8 servings**

**Slow Cooker** 4- to 5-quart • **Prep Time** 15 min • **Cook Time** Low 7 to 9 hr

1 medium onion, sliced

2-pound pork boneless loin roast

1 package (8 ounces) mixed dried fruit (1 1/2 cups)

1/2 cup apple juice

1/2 teaspoon salt

1/2 teaspoon ground nutmeg

1/4 teaspoon ground cinnamon

*1.* Place onion in 4- to 5-quart slow cooker. Place pork on onion, then top pork with fruit.

*2.* Mix remaining ingredients and pour over fruit.

*3.* Cover and cook on low heat setting 7 to 9 hours or until pork is tender. Serve fruit mixture over pork.

**1 Serving:**
Calories 225 (Calories from Fat 65);
Fat 7g (Saturated 2g); Cholesterol 50mg;
Sodium 180mg; Carbohydrate 22g
(Dietary Fiber 3g); Protein 19g

**% Daily Value:**
Vitamin A 6%; Vitamin C 2%; Calcium 2%;
Iron 8%

**Diet Exchanges:**
2 1/2 Lean Meat, 1 1/2 Fruit

*Betty's Success Tip* Check that the package of dried fruit contains large pieces of fruit, such as slices of peaches, apples, pears and apricots. Diced dried fruit is also available, but the pieces are too small, so they overcook and become part of the sauce during the long, slow cooking.

*Ingredient Substitution* Apple juice enhances the flavors of the dried fruit and pork. You can also use apricot nectar or orange juice.

Roast Pork with Fruit

# Pork and Potatoes with Rosemary

**Slow Cooker** 4- to 6-quart • **Prep Time** 20 min • **Cook Time** Low 8 to 9 hr

1 pound medium red potatoes, cut into fourths

1 cup baby-cut carrots

3 pound pork boneless loin roast

3 tablespoons Dijon mustard

2 tablespoons chopped fresh or 1 1/2 teaspoons dried rosemary leaves, crumbled

1 teaspoon chopped fresh or 1/2 teaspoon dried thyme leaves

1 teaspoon salt

1/2 teaspoon pepper

1 small onion, finely chopped (1/4 cup)

1 1/2 cups beef broth

*1.* Arrange potatoes and carrots around outer edge in 4- to 6-quart slow cooker.

*2.* Remove excess fat from pork. Mix mustard, rosemary, thyme, salt and pepper; spread evenly over pork. Place pork in slow cooker (it will overlap vegetables slightly).

*3.* Sprinkle onion over pork. Pour broth evenly over pork and vegetables. Cover and cook on low heat setting 8 to 9 hours or until pork and vegetables are tender.

*4.* Remove pork and vegetables from slow cooker, using slotted spoon. Slice pork. To serve, spoon juices from slow cooker over pork and vegetables.

**1 Serving:**
Calories 440 (Calories from Fat 160);
Fat 18g (Saturated 6g); Cholesterol 145mg;
Sodium 850mg; Carbohydrate 19g
(Dietary Fiber 2g); Protein 53g

**% Daily Value:**
Vitamin A 32%; Vitamin C 10%; Calcium 4%;
Iron 16%

**Diet Exchanges:**
1 Starch, 6 Lean Meat, 1 Vegetable

*Betty's Success Tip*   If your red potatoes are the small variety, you're better off cutting them in half so they won't overcook.

*Finishing Touch*   To make gravy, you can thicken the pork juices with 2 tablespoons of cornstarch mixed with 1/4 cup of cold water. Shake the cornstarch mixture in a covered container, and heat it with the pork juices in a saucepan on the stove until thickened.

Pork and Potatoes with Rosemary

# Pork Chop Supper

**Slow Cooker** 3 1/2- to 6-quart • **Prep Time** 15 min • **Cook Time** Low 6 to 7 hr • **Finishing Cook Time** Low 15 min

6 pork loin or rib chops, 1/2 inch thick

6 medium new potatoes (about 1 1/2 pounds), cut into eighths

1 can (10 3/4 ounces) condensed cream of mushroom soup

1 can (4 ounces) mushroom pieces and stems, drained

2 tablespoons dry white wine

1/4 teaspoon dried thyme leaves

1/2 teaspoon garlic powder

1/2 teaspoon Worcestershire sauce

3 tablespoons all-purpose flour

1 tablespoon diced pimientos

1 package (10 ounces) frozen green peas, rinsed and drained

*1.* Spray 10-inch nonstick skillet with cooking spray; heat over medium-high heat. Cook pork in skillet, turning once, until brown.

*2.* Place potatoes in 3 1/2- to 6-quart slow cooker. Mix soup, mushrooms, wine, thyme, garlic powder, Worcestershire sauce and flour; spoon half of soup mixture over potatoes. Place pork on potatoes; cover with remaining soup mixture.

*3.* Cover and cook on low heat setting 6 to 7 hours or until pork is tender. Remove pork; keep warm. Stir pimientos and peas into slow cooker. Cover and cook on low heat setting about 15 minutes or until peas are tender. Serve with pork.

**1 Serving:**
Calories 275 (Calories from Fat 100); Fat 11g (Saturated 4g); Cholesterol 65mg; Sodium 520mg; Carbohydrate 21g (Dietary Fiber 4g); Protein 27g

**% Daily Value:**
Vitamin A 4%; Vitamin C 8%; Calcium 4%; Iron 14%

**Diet Exchanges:**
1 Starch, 3 Lean Meat, 1 Vegetable

*Ingredient Substitution* White wine adds a great flavor, but if you don't have any on hand, you can use apple juice. Golden cream of mushroom, cream of chicken or cream of celery soup can be used instead of the cream of mushroom.

# Saucy Barbecued Ribs

**Slow Cooker** 5- to 6-quart • **Prep Time** 10 min • **Cook Time** Low 8 to 9 hr • **Finishing Cook Time** Low 1 hr

3 1/2 pounds pork loin back ribs or pork spareribs

1/2 teaspoon salt

1/4 teaspoon pepper

1/2 cup water

2/3 cup barbecue sauce

*1.* Spray inside of 5- to 6-quart slow cooker with cooking spray.

*2.* Cut ribs into 2- or 3-rib portions. Place ribs in slow cooker; sprinkle with salt and pepper. Pour water into slow cooker.

*3.* Cover and cook on low heat setting 8 to 9 hours or until ribs are tender. Remove ribs. Drain and discard liquid.

*4.* Pour barbecue sauce into shallow bowl; dip ribs into sauce. Place ribs in slow cooker. Pour any remaining sauce over ribs. Cover and cook on low heat setting 1 hour.

**1 Serving:**
Calories 520 (Calories from Fat 350);
Fat 39g (Saturated 14g); Cholesterol 155mg;
Sodium 540mg; Carbohydrate 4g
(Dietary Fiber 0g); Protein 38g

**% Daily Value:**
Vitamin A 2%; Vitamin C 0%; Calcium 6%;
Iron 14%

**Diet Exchanges:**
5 High-Fat Meat, 1 Vegetable

*Ingredient Substitution*   You may find this surprising, but use 1/2 cup cola instead of water. Cola adds a wonderful sweetness to the ribs. Try it for a little variety.

*Serving Suggestion*   Stop at the store and pick up coleslaw or baked beans for an easy, southern barbecued rib dinner.

# Easy French Dip Sandwiches

**Slow Cooker** 3 1/2- to 6-quart • **Prep Time** 5 min • **Cook Time** Low 8 to 10 hr

3 pound fresh beef brisket (not corned beef)

1 package (1.3 ounces) dry onion soup mix

1 can (10 1/2 ounces) condensed beef broth

8 mini baguettes or sandwich buns

*1.* Place beef in 3 1/2- to 6-quart slow cooker. Mix dry soup mix and beef broth; pour over beef.

*2.* Cover and cook on low heat setting 8 to 10 hours or until beef is tender.

*3.* Skim fat from liquid. Remove beef; cut across grain into thin slices. Cut each baguette horizontally in half. Fill baguettes with beef; cut in half. Serve with broth for dipping.

**1 Sandwich:**
Calories 270 (Calories from Fat 90);
Fat 10g (Saturated 3g); Cholesterol 60mg;
Sodium 620mg; Carbohydrate 20g
(Dietary Fiber 1g); Protein 26g

**% Daily Value:**
Vitamin A 0%; Vitamin C 0%; Calcium 6%;
Iron 16%

**Diet Exchanges:**
1 Starch, 3 Lean Meat, 1/2 Fat

*Serving Suggestion* If you're looking for an easy recipe for a family get-together, this is it! Serve with frosty mugs of root beer, deli potato salad and sliced fresh fruit.

Easy French Dip Sandwiches

# Sloppy Joes

**Slow Cooker** 3 1/2- to 6-quart • **Prep Time** 15 min • **Cook Time** Low 7 to 9 hr • **Finishing Cook Time** High 15 min

3 pounds ground beef

1 large onion, coarsely chopped (1 cup)

3/4 cup chopped celery

1 cup barbecue sauce

1 can (26 1/2 ounces) sloppy joe sauce

24 hamburger buns

*1.* Cook beef and onion in Dutch oven over medium heat, stirring occasionally, until beef is brown; drain.

*2.* Mix beef mixture and remaining ingredients except buns in 3 1/2- to 6-quart slow cooker.

*3.* Cover and cook on low heat setting 7 to 9 hours or until vegetables are tender.

*4.* Uncover and cook on high heat setting 15 minutes or until desired consistency. Stir well before serving. Fill buns with beef mixture.

**1 Sandwich:**
Calories 155 (Calories from Fat 80); Fat 9g (Saturated 3g); Cholesterol 30mg; Sodium 270mg; Carbohydrate 8g (Dietary Fiber 1g); Protein 11g

**% Daily Value:**
Vitamin A 2%; Vitamin C 4%; Calcium 2%; Iron 6%

**Diet Exchanges:**
1 High-Fat Meat, 2 Vegetable

*Ingredient Substitution*    Stir 1 cup drained sauerkraut into the mixture before serving. It will add a nice flavor twist, and no one will guess the "secret ingredient."

*Serving Suggestion*    You can serve this tasty beef mixture over hot cooked rice or pasta rather than using as a sandwich filling. Or spoon it over tortilla chips and top each serving with shredded lettuce and shredded cheese.

# Pulled-Pork Fajitas

**Slow Cooker** 3 1/2- to 6-quart • **Prep Time** 10 min • **Cook Time** Low 8 to 10 hr

2 1/2 pound pork boneless loin roast

1 medium onion, thinly sliced

2 cups barbecue sauce

3/4 cup salsa

3 tablespoons chili powder

1 tablespoon Mexican seasoning

9 flour tortillas (8 to 10 inches in diameter)

*1.* Remove excess fat from pork. Place pork in 3 1/2- to 6-quart slow cooker; arrange onion on top. Mix remaining ingredients except tortillas; pour over pork.

*2.* Cover and cook on low heat setting 8 to 10 hours or until pork is very tender.

*3.* Remove pork; place on large plate. Use 2 forks to pull pork into shreds. Pour sauce into bowl; stir in pork. Spoon filling onto tortillas; roll up.

**1 Serving:**
Calories 395 (Calories from Fat 135);
Fat 15g (Saturated 4g); Cholesterol 80mg;
Sodium 790mg; Carbohydrate 35g
(Dietary Fiber 4g); Protein 34g

**% Daily Value:**
Vitamin A 14%; Vitamin C 8%; Calcium 8%;
Iron 20%

**Diet Exchanges:**
2 Starch, 4 Lean Meat, 1 Vegetable

*Betty's Success Tip*    Leftover shredded pork can be stored in the refrigerator for up to 4 days or frozen up to 4 months, and used for tacos, enchiladas and burrito fillings.

*Ingredient Substitution*    You can use a 2 1/2-pound beef boneless chuck roast instead of the pork roast.

# Chapter 2

# Delicious Chicken and Turkey Dinners

Photos, clockwise from top left: Spanish Chicken (page 32), Savory Chicken and Vegetables (page 38), Home-Style Turkey Dinner (page 46), Mexican Chicken with Green Chili Rice (page 30)

# Mexican Chicken with Green Chili Rice

**Slow Cooker** 3 1/2- to 6-quart • **Prep Time** 15 min • **Cook Time** Low 7 to 8 hr

1 medium butternut squash, peeled, seeded and cut into 2-inch pieces

1 medium green bell pepper, cut into 1-inch pieces

4 skinless, boneless chicken breast halves (about 1 pound), each cut into 3 pieces

1 can (14 1/2 ounces) stewed tomatoes, undrained

1/2 cup salsa

1/4 cup raisins

1/4 teaspoon ground cinnamon

1/4 teaspoon ground cumin

3 cups hot cooked rice, for serving

1 can (4 ounces) chopped green chilies, drained

**1.** Layer squash, bell pepper and chicken in 3 1/2- to 6-quart slow cooker. Mix tomatoes, salsa, raisins, cinnamon and cumin; pour over chicken mixture.

**2.** Cover and cook on low heat setting 7 to 8 hours or until squash is tender and juice of chicken is no longer pink when centers of thickest pieces are cut.

**3.** Mix rice and chilies.

**4.** Remove chicken and vegetables from cooker, using slotted spoon. Serve on rice. Stir sauce in cooker; spoon over chicken and vegetables.

*Ingredient Substitution*    Cumin, a tiny seed the size and shape of a caraway seed, is the dried fruit of the parsley family. This aromatic spice is a popular seasoning for Mexican cooking and is also one of the spices in chili powder. You can use 1/4 teaspoon chili powder to replace the ground cumin in this chicken dish.

*Finishing Touch*    If you like your bell pepper with a bit of crunch, add it to the mixture for the last 15 minutes of cooking. Uncover and cook on high heat setting about 15 minutes or until pepper is crisp-tender.

**1 Serving:**
Calories 400 (Calories from Fat 45); Fat 5g (Saturated 1g); Cholesterol 75mg; Sodium 490mg; Carbohydrate 61g (Dietary Fiber 4g); Protein 32g

**% Daily Value:**
Vitamin A 60%; Vitamin C 62%; Calcium 10%; Iron 22%

**Diet Exchanges:**
3 Starch, 2 Lean Meat, 3 Vegetable

Mexican Chicken with Green Chili Rice

# Spanish Chicken

**Slow Cooker** 3 1/2- to 4-quart • **Prep Time** 15 min • **Cook Time** Low 6 to 8 hr

1 large onion, chopped (1 cup)

2 cloves garlic, finely chopped

1 large red bell pepper, chopped
(1 1/2 cups)

1 teaspoon dried oregano leaves

1/2 to 1 teaspoon crushed
red pepper

1 pound turkey Italian sausages,
cut into 1-inch pieces

1 3/4 pounds boneless, skinless
chicken breast halves, cut into
1-inch pieces

1 can (28 ounces) diced tomatoes,
undrained

1 can (6 ounces) tomato paste

1 can (14 ounces) artichoke heart
quarters, drained

1 can (4 ounces) sliced ripe olives,
drained

3 cups hot cooked rice

*1.* Mix all ingredients except artichoke hearts, olives and rice in
3 1/2- to 4-quart slow cooker.

*2.* Cover and cook on low heat setting 6 to 8 hours or until sausages
and chicken are no longer pink in center. Stir in artichoke hearts
and olives; heat through. Serve with cooked rice.

**1 Serving:**
Calories 490 (Calories from Fat 145);
Fat 16g (Saturated 4g); Cholesterol 115mg;
Sodium 1320mg; Carbohydrate 48g
(Dietary Fiber 8g); Protein 47g

**% Daily Value:**
Vitamin A 36%; Vitamin C 76%; Calcium 14%;
Iron 30%

**Diet Exchanges:**
3 Starch, 5 Very Lean Meat, 1 Vegetable,
1 Fat

*Betty's Success Tip*   Turkey sausage is low in fat but still is high in flavor! Check the label on the sausage to make sure it is made with turkey
breast, which is lower in fat than turkey sausage made with dark meat.

*Ingredient Substitution*   For an authentic flavor, use pitted
Kalamata or Greek olives instead of the ripe olives.

Spanish Chicken

# Creamy Chicken Pot Pie

**Slow Cooker** 3 1/2- to 6-quart • **Prep Time** 20 min • **Cook Time** Low 4 hr • **Finishing Cook Time** High 1 hour 10 min

1 envelope (0.87 to 1.2-ounces) chicken gravy mix

1 can (10 1/2 ounces) condensed chicken broth

1 pound skinless, boneless chicken breasts, cut into 1-inch pieces

1 bag (16 ounces) frozen stew vegetables, thawed and drained

1 jar (4 ounces) sliced mushrooms, drained

1/2 cup sour cream

1 tablespoon all-purpose flour

1 1/2 cups Bisquick® Original or Reduced Fat baking mix

4 medium green onions, chopped (1/4 cup)

1/2 cup milk

1 cup frozen green peas, thawed

*1.* Mix gravy mix and broth in 3 1/2- to 6-quart slow cooker until smooth. Stir in chicken, stew vegetables and mushrooms.

*2.* Cover and cook on low heat setting about 4 hours or until chicken is tender.

*3.* Mix sour cream and flour. Stir sour cream mixture into chicken mixture. Cover and cook on high heat setting 20 minutes.

*4.* Mix baking mix and onions; stir in milk just until moistened. Stir in peas. Drop dough by rounded tablespoonfuls onto chicken-vegetable mixture.

*5.* Cover and cook on high heat setting 45 to 50 minutes or until toothpick inserted in center of topping comes out clean. Serve immediately.

*Betty's Success Tip*   A bag of frozen vegetables for stew—potatoes, carrots, onions and peas—is really handy for this recipe. The size the vegetables are cut varies from brand to brand. The good news is that both the small and medium size pieces of vegetables all were done by the end of the cooking time.

***Serving Suggestion***   What's so great about a pot pie is that it is a complete meal—chicken, vegetables and bread—all in one. Add a little crispness and color to the meal by serving a leafy green salad. Toss a bag of romaine salad greens with a drained can of mandarin orange segments and your favorite poppy seed dressing. Sprinkle each serving with some toasted sliced almonds.

**1 Serving:**
Calories 535 (Calories from Fat 155); Fat 17g (Saturated 7g); Cholesterol 95mg; Sodium 2100mg; Carbohydrate 56g (Dietary Fiber 5g); Protein 45g

**% Daily Value:**
Vitamin A 42%; Vitamin C 6%; Calcium 18%; Iron 20%

**Diet Exchanges:**
3 Starch, 4 Lean Meat, 2 Vegetable, 1 Fat

# Mango Chutney Chicken Curry

**Slow Cooker** 3 1/2- to 4-quart • **Prep Time** 20 min • **Cook Time** Low 6 to 7 hr

4 skinless, bone-in chicken breast halves (about 7 ounces each)

1 can (15 to 16 ounces) garbanzo beans, rinsed and drained

1 small onion, thinly sliced

1 small red bell pepper, chopped (1/2 cup)

1 cup snap pea pods

3/4 cup water

2 tablespoons cornstarch

1 1/2 teaspoons curry powder

1/4 teaspoon salt

1/4 teaspoon pepper

1 jar (9 ounces) mango chutney

4 cups hot cooked rice or couscous, for serving

*1.* Layer chicken, beans, onion, bell pepper and pea pods in 3 1/2- to 4-quart slow cooker. Mix remaining ingredients except rice; pour into cooker.

*2.* Cover and cook on low heat setting 6 to 7 hours or until vegetables are tender and juice of chicken is no longer pink when centers of thickest pieces are cut.

*3.* Serve chicken mixture over rice.

**1 Serving:**
Calories 600 (Calories from Fat 65); Fat 7g (Saturated 2g); Cholesterol 75mg; Sodium 410mg; Carbohydrate 103g (Dietary Fiber 11g); Protein 42g

**% Daily Value:**
Vitamin A 12%; Vitamin C 42%; Calcium 10%; Iron 38%

**Diet Exchanges:**
3 Starch, 4 Very Lean Meat, 2 Vegetable, 3 Fruit

*Ingredient Substitution*    Chutney is a spicy mixture of fruit, vinegar, sugar and spices. It can vary in texture from chunky to smooth and in spiciness from mild to hot. We liked the sweetness of the mango chutney, but you can try your favorite chutney in this curried delight.

*Finishing Touch*    Serve small bowls of traditional curry dish toppers, such as toasted shredded coconut, chopped peanuts and raisins. The saltiness of the peanuts and the sweetness of the coconut and raisins enhance the flavors of the curry powder and chutney. Serve additional mango chutney to spoon alongside the chicken and rice.

# Chicken, Stuffing and Sweet Potato Dinner

**6 servings**

**Slow Cooker** 5- to 6-quart • **Prep Time** 20 min • **Cook Time** Low 4 to 6 hr • **Finishing Cook Time** Low 15 to 20 min

3 pounds bone-in chicken pieces, skin removed

1 can (10 3/4 ounces) condensed cream of chicken with herbs soup

4 sweet potatoes or yams, peeled and cut into 1/2-inch slices

1 package (6 ounces) stuffing mix for chicken

1 1/4 cups water

1/4 cup margarine or butter, melted

1 cup frozen (thawed) cut green beans

**1.** Place chicken in 5- to 6-quart slow cooker. Spoon soup over chicken. Top with sweet potatoes. Mix stuffing mix, water and margarine; spoon over sweet potatoes.

**2.** Cover and cook on low heat setting 4 to 6 hours or until potatoes are tender and juice of chicken is no longer pink when centers of thickest pieces are cut.

**3.** Sprinkle green beans over stuffing. Cover and cook on low heat setting 15 to 20 minutes or until beans are tender.

**1 Serving:**
Calories 520 (Calories from Fat 205);
Fat 23g (Saturated 6g); Cholesterol 150mg;
Sodium 740mg; Carbohydrate 30g
(Dietary Fiber 3g); Protein 51g

**% Daily Value:**
Vitamin A 100%; Vitamin C 16%; Calcium 6%;
Iron 16%

**Diet Exchanges:**
2 Starch, 6 1/2 Lean Meat

*Betty's Success Tip*  The stuffing mix for chicken is the already-flavored bread crumb mixture that comes in a box. All the seasoning are included, and you just add the water and the butter—it's that easy! You can use your family's favorite chicken pieces, such as legs, thighs, breasts or a mixture of all three, so everyone gets his or her favorite "pick of the day."

*Ingredient Substitution*  The herbs in the cream of chicken soup make a nicely seasoned one-dish meal. You also can use your favorite cream soup, such as golden onion or broccoli.

# Chicken Legs with Herbed Onion Sauce

**Slow Cooker** 3 1/2- to 6-quart · **Prep Time** 15 min · **Cook Time** Low 4 to 5 hr

10 chicken drumsticks (about 2 pounds), skin removed

2 cups frozen (thawed) pearl onions

1/4 cup dry white wine or chicken broth

1/4 cup canned evaporated milk

2 tablespoons chopped fresh parsley or 2 teaspoons parsley flakes

1 teaspoon dried tarragon leaves

1/4 teaspoon salt

1/4 teaspoon dried rosemary leaves, crumbled

1 can (10 3/4 ounces) condensed cream of chicken soup

*1.* Place chicken in 3 1/2- to 6-quart slow cooker. Mix remaining ingredients; pour over chicken.

*2.* Cover and cook on low heat setting 4 to 5 hours or until juice of chicken is no longer pink when centers of thickest pieces are cut.

**1 Serving:**
Calories 230 (Calories from Fat 70); Fat 8g (Saturated 3g); Cholesterol 105mg; Sodium 640mg; Carbohydrate 11g (Dietary Fiber 1g); Protein 29g

**% Daily Value:**
Vitamin A 4%; Vitamin C 4%; Calcium 8%; Iron 16%

**Diet Exchanges:**
3 1/2 Very Lean Meat, 2 Vegetable, 1 Fat

*Ingredient Substitution*   Those fresh little pearl onions can be time-consuming to peel, so using the frozen thawed ones saves you a lot of time. If you don't have pearl onions in the freezer, you can slice and use a large yellow or white onion.

*Finishing Touch*   Serve all that wonderfully flavored sauce spooned over the chicken legs. Tuck a perky sprig of fresh tarragon or rosemary next to the chicken, or sprinkle a little chopped fresh parsley over the top for that special touch.

# Savory Chicken and Vegetables

**8 servings**

**Slow Cooker** 5- to 6-quart • **Prep Time** 20 min • **Cook Time** Low 8 to 10 hr • **Finishing Cook Time** High 30 min

8 boneless, skinless chicken thighs (about 1 1/2 pounds)

2 cups chicken broth

1 teaspoon salt

1/4 teaspoon pepper

8 ounces pearl onions

6 slices bacon, cooked and crumbled

2 cloves garlic, finely chopped

Bouquet Garni (right)

1 bag (1 pound) baby-cut carrots

1 pound small whole button mushrooms

2 tablespoons all-purpose flour

2 tablespoons cold water

*1.* Place chicken in 5- to 6-quart slow cooker. Add remaining ingredients except mushrooms, flour and water.

*2.* Cover and cook on low heat setting 8 to 10 hours or until juice of chicken is no longer pink when centers of thickest pieces are cut.

*3.* Remove any fat from surface. Remove Bouquet Garni. Stir in mushrooms. Mix flour and water; stir into chicken mixture.

*4.* Cover and cook on high heat setting 30 minutes or until mixture thickens.

## Bouquet Garni

Tie 4 sprigs parsley, 2 bay leaves and 1 teaspoon dried thyme leaves in cheesecloth bag or place in tea ball.

**1 Serving:**
Calories 190 (Calories from Fat 70);
Fat 8g (Saturated 3g); Cholesterol 45mg;
Sodium 530mg; Carbohydrate 13g
(Dietary Fiber 3g); Protein 19g

**% Daily Value:**
Vitamin A 88%; Vitamin C 6%; Calcium 4%;
Iron 14%

**Diet Exchanges:**
3 Lean Meat, 3 Vegetable

*Ingredient Substitution*   Use 1 1/4 cups of red wine and 3/4 cup of chicken broth instead of 2 cups of chicken broth. Sprinkle with coarsely ground fresh black pepper.

*Serving Suggestion*   Be sure to serve this saucy dish in shallow soup bowls, and sprinkle a little chopped parsley on top for color and added flavor.

Savory Chicken and Vegetables

# Turkey with Wild Rice, Squash and Cranberries

**6 servings**

**Slow Cooker** 4- to 5-quart • **Prep Time** 15 min • **Cook Time** Low 7 to 9 hr

3/4 cup uncooked wild rice, rinsed and drained

1 medium butternut squash, peeled, seeded and cut into 1-inch pieces

1 medium onion, cut into wedges

1 1/4 pounds turkey breast tenderloins

1/2 teaspoon dried thyme leaves

1/2 teaspoon salt

1/2 teaspoon pepper

3 cups chicken broth

1/2 cup dried cranberries

**1.** Place wild rice in 4- to 5-quart slow cooker. Top rice with squash, onion and turkey. Sprinkle with thyme, salt and pepper.

**2.** Pour chicken broth over all ingredients. Cover and cook on low heat setting 7 to 9 hours or until rice is tender. Stir in cranberries.

**1 Serving:**
Calories 280 (Calories from Fat 20);
Fat 2g (Saturated 1g); Cholesterol 60mg;
Sodium 770mg; Carbohydrate 43g
(Dietary Fiber 7g); Protein 29g

**% Daily Value:**
Vitamin A 88%; Vitamin C 26%; Calcium 8%;
Iron 16%

**Diet Exchanges:**
2 Starch, 2 Very Lean Meat, 3 Vegetable

*Ingredient Substitution* Butternut squash resembles the shape of a lightbulb or pear—it's wider at one end than the other. It usually weighs between 2 and 3 pounds and has a golden yellow to camel-colored shell. You can also use about 2 pounds of other winter squash, such as Hubbard or buttercup.

# Southwestern Turkey

**Slow Cooker** 2 1/2- to 4-quart • **Prep Time** 15 min • **Cook Time** Low 4 to 6 hr

1 tablespoon olive or vegetable oil

1 1/4 pounds turkey breast tenderloins, cut into 1-inch cubes

1 can (14 1/2 ounces) diced tomatoes with Mexican seasoning, undrained

1/2 medium green bell pepper, thinly sliced

1 tablespoon chili powder

2 tablespoons lime juice

1 teaspoon sugar

1/2 teaspoon salt

*1.* Heat oil in 12-inch skillet over medium-high heat. Cook turkey in oil 4 to 6 minutes, stirring occasionally, until brown. Place turkey in 2 1/2- to 4-quart slow cooker.

*2.* Mix remaining ingredients; pour over turkey.

*3.* Cover and cook on low heat setting 4 to 6 hours or until turkey is no longer pink in center.

**1 Serving:**
Calories 125 (Calories from Fat 20);
Fat 3g (Saturated 0g); Cholesterol 60mg;
Sodium 350mg; Carbohydrate 5g
(Dietary Fiber 1g); Protein 23g

**% Daily Value:**
Vitamin A 8%; Vitamin C 16%; Calcium 4%;
Iron 10%

**Diet Exchanges:**
3 Very Lean Meat, 1 Vegetable

*Serving Suggestion*　Just get home and know everyone is hungry? Make some boil-in-the-bag rice as a bed for this yummy turkey. It'll take about 15 minutes to cook. Pop some whole kernel corn into the microwave for a pleasing side dish. The next thing you know, you'll have dinner on the table before the family can ask, "What's for dinner?"

*Finishing Touch*　Cilantro is a popular herb used in many southwestern recipes. It has a pungent flavor and aroma with a cool, minty overtone. Sprinkle a couple tablespoons of chopped fresh cilantro over the turkey just before serving to add extra flavor to this dish.

# Turkey Drumsticks with Plum Sauce

**Slow Cooker** 5- to 6-quart • **Prep Time** 10 min • **Cook Time** Low 8 to 10 hr • **Finishing Cook Time** High 15 to 20 min

4 turkey drumsticks (2 1/2 to 3 pounds), skin removed

1/2 teaspoon salt

1/4 teaspoon pepper

2/3 cup plum sauce

1/3 cup sliced green onions

1 tablespoon soy sauce

1 tablespoon cornstarch

1 tablespoon cold water

3 cups hot cooked rice, for serving

*1.* Sprinkle turkey with salt and pepper. Place turkey in 5- to 6-quart slow cooker. Mix plum sauce, green onions and soy sauce; pour over turkey.

*2.* Cover and cook on low heat setting 8 to 10 hours or until juice of turkey is no longer pink when centers of thickest pieces are cut.

*3.* Remove turkey from cooker. Cover with aluminum foil to keep warm.

*4.* Remove any fat from sauce. Mix cornstarch and water; stir into sauce.

*5.* Cover and cook on high heat setting 15 to 20 minutes or until sauce has thickened. Cut turkey from drumsticks. Serve with sauce and rice.

**1 Serving:**
Calories 510 (Calories from Fat 80);
Fat 9g (Saturated 3g); Cholesterol 210mg;
Sodium 680mg; Carbohydrate 50g
(Dietary Fiber 1g); Protein 58g

**% Daily Value:**
Vitamin A 0%; Vitamin C 2%; Calcium 8%;
Iron 36%

**Diet Exchanges:**
3 Starch, 7 Very Lean Meat, 1 Vegetable

*Ingredient Substitution*    Plum sauce is a sweet-and-sour sauce made from plums, apricots, sugar and seasonings. You can find it in the Asian-foods section of the supermarket or at an Asian grocery store. If plum sauce isn't available, use apricot or cherry preserves and it will still be delicious!

*Serving Suggestion*    Keep to the Asian theme by serving this plum-good turkey with crisply cooked pea pods. A fresh salad of assorted melon—cantaloupe, honeydew and watermelon—drizzled lightly with your favorite fruit salad dressing makes a light yet satisfying meal.

Turkey Drumsticks with Plum Sauce

# Simmering Turkey Breast

**Slow Cooker** 5-quart • **Prep Time** 15 min • **Cook Time** Low 8 to 9 hr

6 1/2-pound bone-in turkey breast, thawed if frozen

1 medium onion, chopped (1/2 cup)

1 medium stalk celery, chopped (1/2 cup)

1 bay leaf

1 teaspoon salt

1/2 teaspoon coarsely ground pepper

1 teaspoon chicken bouillon granules

1/2 cup water

1. Remove gravy packet or extra parts from turkey breast. Place onion, celery and bay leaf in cavity of turkey. Place turkey in 5-quart slow cooker.

2. Sprinkle turkey with salt and pepper. Mix bouillon and water until granules are dissolved; pour over turkey.

3. Cover and cook on low heat setting 8 to 9 hours or until juice of turkey is no longer pink when center is cut. Remove bay leaf.

**1 Serving:**
Calories 310 (Calories from Fat 115); Fat 13g (Saturated 4g); Cholesterol 125mg; Sodium 410mg; Carbohydrate 1g (Dietary Fiber 0g); Protein 47g

**% Daily Value:**
Vitamin A 4%; Vitamin C 0%; Calcium 2%; Iron 8%

**Diet Exchanges:**
7 Very Lean Meat, 1 Fat

*Serving Suggestion*    Broccoli spears and a tossed green salad are great side dishes that always go well with turkey.

# Rosemary Turkey and Potatoes

**Slow Cooker** 3 1/2- to 6-quart • **Prep Time** 15 min • **Cook Time** Low 8 to 10 hr

3 medium potatoes, cut into 2-inch pieces

1 package (10 ounces) frozen cut green beans

3 turkey thighs (about 3 pounds), skin removed

1 jar (12 ounces) home-style turkey gravy

2 tablespoons all-purpose flour

1 teaspoon parsley flakes

1/2 teaspoon dried rosemary leaves, crumbled

1/8 teaspoon pepper

*1.* Layer potatoes, green beans and turkey in 3 1/2- to 6-quart slow cooker. Mix remaining ingredients until smooth; pour over mixture in cooker.

*2.* Cover and cook on low heat setting 8 to 10 hours or until juice of turkey is no longer pink when centers of thickest pieces are cut.

*3.* Remove turkey and vegetables from cooker, using slotted spoon. Stir sauce; serve with turkey and vegetables.

**1 Serving:**
Calories 335 (Calories from Fat 70);
Fat 8g (Saturated 3g); Cholesterol 155mg;
Sodium 450mg; Carbohydrate 26g
(Dietary Fiber 4g); Protein 44g

**% Daily Value:**
Vitamin A 100%; Vitamin C 16%; Calcium 8%;
Iron 26%

**Diet Exchanges:**
1 Starch, 5 Very Lean Meat, 2 Vegetable,
1/2 Fat

*Betty's Success Tip* Potatoes sometimes take longer to cook than other vegetables or meats in a slow cooker. By putting them into the cooker first, they are in liquid during the long cooking time and will be done in the same time as the other ingredients.

# Home-Style Turkey Dinner

**Slow Cooker** 3 1/2- to 6-quart • **Prep Time** 15 min • **Cook Time** Low 8 to 10 hours • **Finishing Cook Time** Low 30 min

3 medium Yukon gold potatoes, cut into 2-inch pieces

3 turkey thighs (about 3 pounds), skin removed

1 jar (12 ounces) home-style turkey gravy

2 tablespoons all-purpose flour

1 teaspoon parsley flakes

1/2 teaspoon dried thyme leaves

1/8 teaspoon pepper

1 bag (1 pound) frozen baby bean and carrot blend, thawed and drained

*1.* Place potatoes in 3 1/2- to 6-quart slow cooker; arrange turkey on top. Mix remaining ingredients except vegetables until smooth; pour over mixture in slow cooker.

*2.* Cover and cook on low heat setting 8 to 10 hours or until juice of turkey is no longer pink when centers of thickest pieces are cut. Stir in vegetables.

*3.* Cover and cook on low heat setting about 30 minutes or until vegetables are tender.

*4.* Remove turkey and vegetables from slow cooker, using slotted spoon. Stir sauce; serve with turkey and vegetables.

**1 Serving:**
Calories 335 (Calories from Fat 70); Fat 8g (Saturated 3g); Cholesterol 155mg; Sodium 450mg; Carbohydrate 26g (Dietary Fiber 4g); Protein 44g

**% Daily Value:**
Vitamin A 100%; Vitamin C 16%; Calcium 8%; Iron 26%

**Diet Exchanges:**
1 Starch, 5 Very Lean Meat, 2 Vegetable, 1/2 Fat

*Ingredient Substitution*   If you love sweet potatoes, use 3 medium sweet potatoes, peeled and cut into 2-inch pieces, instead of the Yukon gold potatoes.

Home-Style Turkey Dinner

# Chapter 3

# Simmering Soups, Stews and Chilis

Photos, clockwise from top left: Grandma's Chicken Noodle Soup (page 50), Italian Spaghetti Sauce (page 66), Beef Stew with Sun-Dried Tomatoes (page 60), Colombian Beef and Sweet Potato Stew (page 58)

# Grandma's Chicken Noodle Soup

**6 servings**

**Slow Cooker** 3 1/2- to 4-quart • **Prep Time** 30 min • **Cook Time** Low 6 1/2 to 7 hr • **Finishing Cook Time** Low 10 min

3/4 pound boneless, skinless chicken thighs, cut into 1-inch pieces

2 medium stalks celery (with leaves), sliced (1 1/4 cups)

1 large carrot, chopped (3/4 cup)

1 medium onion, chopped (1/2 cup)

1 can (14 1/2 ounces) diced tomatoes, undrained

1 can (14 1/2 ounces) chicken broth

1 teaspoon dried thyme leaves

1 package (10 ounces) frozen green peas

1 cup frozen home-style egg noodles (from 12-ounce package)

*1.* Spray 10-inch skillet with cooking spray; heat over medium heat. Cook chicken in skillet 5 minutes, stirring frequently, until brown.

*2.* Mix chicken and remaining ingredients except peas and noodles in 3 1/2- to 4-quart slow cooker.

*3.* Cover and cook on low heat setting 6 1/2 to 7 hours or until chicken is no longer pink in center. Stir in peas and noodles; cook about 10 minutes longer or until noodles are tender.

**1 Serving:**
Calories 215 (Calories from fat 65);
Fat 7g (Saturated 2g); Cholesterol 45mg;
Sodium 1260mg; Carbohydrate 20g
(Dietary Fiber 4g); Protein 22g

**% Daily Value:**
Vitamin A 22%; Vitamin C 14%; Calcium 6%;
Iron 18%

**Diet Exchanges:**
1 Starch, 2 Very Lean Meat, 1 Vegetable,
1 Fat

*Ingredient Substitution*   We love the old-fashioned flavor of the home-style noodles, but if they aren't available, use 1 cup of uncooked fine egg noodles or instant rice.

*Finishing Touch*   Stir in 1 tablespoon chopped fresh parsley just before serving.

Grandma's Chicken Noodle Soup

# Vegetable-Beef Barley Soup

**10 servings**

**Slow Cooker** 3 1/2- to 6-quart • **Prep Time** 20 min • **Cook Time** Low 8 to 9 hr

1 1/2 pounds beef stew meat

1 small bell pepper, chopped (1/2 cup)

3/4 cup green beans, cut into 1-inch pieces

3/4 cup chopped onion

2/3 cup uncooked barley

2/3 cup fresh whole kernel corn

1 1/2 cups water

1 teaspoon salt

1 teaspoon chopped fresh or 1/2 teaspoon dried thyme leaves

1/4 teaspoon pepper

2 cans (14 1/2 ounces each) ready-to-serve beef broth

2 cans (14 1/2 ounces each) diced tomatoes with garlic, undrained

1 can (8 ounces) tomato sauce

*1.* Mix all ingredients in 3 1/2- to 6-quart slow cooker.

*2.* Cover and cook on low heat setting 8 to 9 hours or until vegetables and barley are tender.

*Ingredient Substitution*　If you can't find the canned diced tomatoes with garlic, use 2 cans diced tomatoes and add 1/2 teaspoon garlic powder. To save time and to make this hearty soup in the winter months, use 3/4 cup frozen cut green beans and 2/3 cup frozen whole kernel corn. Rinse the frozen vegetables under cold running water to separate and partially thaw them before adding to the soup.

*Finishing Touch*　Top this soup with a handful of herb-flavored croutons and a little shredded Parmesan cheese. Bursting with big, juicy chunks of meat, hearty barley and yummy vegetables, this soup is a meal in itself!

**1 Serving:**
Calories 200 (Calories from Fat 65);
Fat 7g (Saturated 3g); Cholesterol 35mg;
Sodium 1000mg; Carbohydrate 22g
(Dietary Fiber 4g); Protein 16g

**% Daily Value:**
Vitamin A 6%; Vitamin C 16%; Calcium 4%;
Iron 14%

**Diet Exchanges:**
1 Starch, 1 1/2 Medium-Fat Meat,
1 Vegetable

# Butternut Squash Soup

**Slow Cooker** 3 1/2- to 4-quart • **Prep Time** 15 min • **Cook Time** Low 6 to 8 hr • **Finishing Cook Time** Low 30 min

2 tablespoons margarine or butter

1 medium onion, chopped
(1/2 cup)

1 butternut squash (2 pounds),
peeled, seeded and cubed

2 cups water

1/2 teaspoon dried marjoram leaves

1/4 teaspoon ground black pepper

1/8 teaspoon ground red pepper
(cayenne)

4 chicken bouillon cubes

1 package (8 ounces) cream cheese,
cubed

*1.* Melt margarine in 10-inch skillet over medium heat. Cook onion in margarine, stirring occasionally, until crisp-tender.

*2.* Mix onion and remaining ingredients except cream cheese in 3 1/2- to 4-quart slow cooker. Cover and cook on low heat setting 6 to 8 hours or until squash is tender.

*3.* Place one-third to one-half of the mixture at a time in blender or food processor. Cover and blend on high speed until smooth. Return mixture to slow cooker; stir in cream cheese. Cover and cook on low heat setting about 30 minutes or until cheese is melted, stirring with wire whisk until smooth.

**1 Serving:**
Calories 235 (Calories from Fat 155);
Fat 17g (Saturated 9g); Cholesterol 40mg;
Sodium 940mg; Carbohydrate 17g
(Dietary Fiber 2g); Protein 5g

**% Daily Value:**
Vitamin A 100%; Vitamin C 16%; Calcium 8%;
Iron 6%

**Diet Exchanges:**
3 Vegetable, 3 1/2 Fat

*Betty's Success Tip* Use a wire whisk to stir the soup after you add the cream cheese so the soup has a smooth consistency.

**Serving Suggestion** Stir in a 1-pound bag of frozen mixed vegetables (thawed and drained) with the cream cheese for a vegetable soup that's totally different, but sure to be delicious!

# Dill Turkey Chowder

**Slow Cooker** 4- to 5-quart • **Prep Time** 15 min • **Cook Time** Low 6 to 8 hr • **Finishing Cook Time** High 20 min

1 pound uncooked turkey breast slices, cut into 1-inch pieces

3/4 teaspoon garlic pepper

1/2 teaspoon salt

6 to 8 new potatoes, cut into 1-inch pieces

1 medium onion, chopped (1/2 cup)

2 medium carrots, sliced (1 cup)

2 teaspoons dried dill weed

2 1/2 cups chicken broth

1 can (15 1/4 ounces) whole kernel corn, drained

1 cup half-and-half

3 tablespoons cornstarch

*1.* Place turkey in 4- to 5-quart slow cooker; sprinkle with garlic pepper and salt. Stir in remaining ingredients except half-and-half and cornstarch.

*2.* Cover and cook on low heat setting 6 to 8 hours or until vegetables are tender.

*3.* Mix half-and-half and cornstarch; gradually stir into chowder until blended. Cover and cook on high heat setting about 20 minutes, stirring occasionally, until thickened.

**1 Serving:**
Calories 265 (Calories from Fat 65);
Fat 7g (Saturated 3g); Cholesterol 55mg;
Sodium 840mg; Carbohydrate 33g
(Dietary Fiber 3g); Protein 21g

**% Daily Value:**
Vitamin A 36%; Vitamin C 12%; Calcium 8%;
Iron 14%

**Diet Exchanges:**
2 Starch, 1 1/2 Very Lean Meat, 1 Vegetable

*Serving Suggestion* Serve this creamy chowder with French bread slices and a large, crisp green salad tossed with your favorite vinaigrette.

Dill Turkey Chowder

# Potato and Ham Chowder

**Slow Cooker** 3 1/2- to 4-quart • **Prep Time** 10 min • **Cook Time** Low 7 hr • **Finishing Cook Time** Low 1 hr

1 package (5 ounces) Betty Crocker® scalloped potatoes

1 cup diced fully cooked ham

4 cups chicken broth

2 medium stalks celery, chopped (1 cup)

1 medium onion, chopped (1/2 cup)

1/8 teaspoon pepper

2 cups half-and-half

1/3 cup all-purpose flour

*1.* Mix potatoes, sauce mix from potatoes, ham, broth, celery, onion and pepper in 3 1/2- to 4-quart slow cooker.

*2.* Cover and cook on low heat setting 7 hours.

*3.* Mix half-and-half and flour. Gradually stir half-and-half mixture into chowder until blended.

*4.* Cover and cook on low heat setting 1 hour, stirring occasionally, until thickened and vegetables are tender.

**1 Serving:**
Calories 340 (Calories from fat 145);
Fat 16g (Saturated 9g); Cholesterol 50mg;
Sodium 1840mg; Carbohydrate 35g
(Dietary Fiber 2g); Protein 16g

**% Daily Value:**
Vitamin A 8%; Vitamin C 2%; Calcium 12%;
Iron 10%

**Diet Exchanges:**
2 Starch, 1 High-Fat Meat, 1 Vegetable,
1 Fat

*Serving Suggestion* This heartwarming chowder can be enjoyed as a meal when paired with warm biscuits. Or serve it as a starter with grilled cheese sandwiches on rye bread.

# Cioppino

**Slow Cooker** 5- to 6-quart • **Prep Time** 20 min • **Cook Time** High 3 to 4 hr • **Finishing Cook Time** Low 30 to 45 min

2 large onions, chopped (2 cups)

2 medium stalks celery, finely chopped

5 cloves garlic, finely chopped

1 can (28 ounces) diced tomatoes, undrained

1 bottle (8 ounces) clam juice

1 can (6 ounces) tomato paste

1/2 cup dry white wine or water

1 tablespoon red wine vinegar

1 tablespoon olive or vegetable oil

2 1/2 teaspoons Italian seasoning

1/4 teaspoon sugar

1/4 teaspoon crushed red pepper

1 dried bay leaf

1 pound firm-fleshed white fish, cut into 1-inch pieces

12 ounces uncooked medium shrimp, peeled and deveined

1 can (6 1/2 ounces) chopped clams with juice, undrained

1 can (6 ounces) crabmeat, drained

1/4 cup chopped fresh parsley

*1.* Mix all ingredients except fish, shrimp, clams, crabmeat and parsley in 5- to 6-quart slow cooker.

*2.* Cover and cook on high heat setting 3 to 4 hours or until vegetables are tender.

*3.* Stir in fish, shrimp, clams and crabmeat. Cover and cook on low heat setting 30 to 45 minutes or until fish flakes easily with fork. Remove bay leaf. Stir in parsley.

**1 Serving:**
Calories 190 (Calories from Fat 35);
Fat 4g (Saturated 1g); Cholesterol 100mg;
Sodium 570mg; Carbohydrate 15g
(Dietary Fiber 3g); Protein 26g

**% Daily Value:**
Vitamin A 18%; Vitamin C 30%; Calcium 12%;
Iron 50%

**Diet Exchanges:**
3 Very Lean Meat, 3 Vegetable

*Betty's Success Tip*    This dish is perfect for those days you stay at home and use your slow cooker. It may require a little more attention, but the results are worth it.

**Serving Suggestion**    Be sure to serve plenty of hearty bread with this fish stew so everyone can sop up every last drop of the wonderful broth in the bottom of the bowl.

# Colombian Beef and Sweet Potato Stew

**6 servings**

**Slow Cooker** 4- to 5-quart • **Prep Time** 15 min • **Cook Time** Low 8 hr • **Finishing Cook Time** Low 15 min

1 pound beef boneless chuck

1/2 teaspoon salt

1/4 teaspoon pepper

1 1/2 teaspoons olive or
   vegetable oil

3 cups 1-inch cubes peeled
   sweet potatoes

2 teaspoons finely chopped garlic

2 whole cloves

1 dried bay leaf

1 stick cinnamon

1 large onion, cut into eighths

1 can (28 ounces) Italian-style
   pear-shaped tomatoes, undrained

8 dried apricots, cut in half

Chopped fresh parsley

*1.* Remove excess fat from beef. Cut beef into 1-inch pieces. Sprinkle beef with salt and pepper. Heat oil in 10-inch skillet over medium-high heat. Cook beef in oil about 5 minutes, stirring occasionally, until brown.

*2.* Mix beef and remaining ingredients except apricots and parsley in 4- to 5-quart slow cooker. Cover and cook on low heat setting about 8 hours or until beef is tender. Stir in apricots.

*3.* Cover and cook on low heat setting about 15 minutes or until apricots are softened. Discard cloves, bay leaf and cinnamon stick. Sprinkle stew with parsley.

**1 Serving:**
Calories 280 (Calories from Fat 90);
Fat 10g (Saturated 3g); Cholesterol 45mg;
Sodium 440mg; Carbohydrate 35g
(Dietary Fiber 6g); Protein 19g

**% Daily Value:**
Vitamin A 100%; Vitamin C 40%; Calcium 8%;
Iron 18%

**Diet Exchanges:**
1 Starch, 2 Lean Meat, 1 Vegetable, 1 Fruit

*Betty's Success Tip* Your family will love the sweet and savory flavor of this Colombian-inspired stew. To save time, purchase already cut-up beef stew meat instead of the beef boneless chuck.

*Serving Suggestion* A great way to enjoy this chunky stew is over fluffy cooked couscous.

Colombian Beef and Sweet Potato Stew

# Beef Stew with Sun-Dried Tomatoes

**6 servings**

**Slow Cooker** 3 1/2- to 6-quart • **Prep Time** 20 min • **Cook Time** Low 8 to 9 hr • **Finishing Cook Time** High 10 to 15 min

1 cup sun-dried tomatoes
   (not oil-packed)

1 1/2 pounds beef stew meat

12 medium new potatoes
   (1 1/2 pounds), cut in half

1 medium onion, cut into 8 wedges

1 bag (8 ounces) baby-cut carrots
   (about 30)

2 cups water

1 1/2 teaspoons seasoned salt

1 bay leaf

1/4 cup cold water

2 tablespoons all-purpose flour

*1.* Soak tomatoes in water as directed on package; drain and coarsely chop.

*2.* Mix tomatoes and remaining ingredients except 1/4 cup water and the flour in 3 1/2- to 6-quart slow cooker.

*3.* Cover and cook on low heat setting 8 to 9 hours (or high heat setting 3 to 5 hours) or until beef and vegetables are tender.

*4.* Mix 1/4 cup water and the flour; gradually stir into beef mixture.

*5.* Cover and cook on high heat setting 10 to 15 minutes or until slightly thickened. Remove bay leaf.

**1 Serving:**
Calories 310 (Calories from Fat 100);
Fat 11g (Saturated 4g); Cholesterol 60mg;
Sodium 600mg; Carbohydrate 34g
(Dietary Fiber 5g); Protein 24g

**% Daily Value:**
Vitamin A 78%; Vitamin C 16%; Calcium 4%;
Iron 24%

**Diet Exchanges:**
2 Starch, 2 Lean Meat, 1 Vegetable, 1/2 Fat

*Ingredient Substitution*   Sun-dried tomatoes add a nice concentrated tomato flavor to the stew. When fresh tomatoes are plentiful, you can add 2 cups chopped fresh tomatoes with the flour mixture instead of using the dried tomatoes.

*Finishing Touch*   Serve stew in bowls, and sprinkle each serving with crumbled crisply cooked bacon and chopped fresh parsley.

Beef Stew with Sun-Dried Tomatoes

# Beef Stew with Shiitake Mushrooms

**Slow Cooker** 3 1/2- to 4-quart • **Prep Time** 20 min • **Cook Time** Low 8 to 9 hr

12 new potatoes (1 1/2 pounds),
cut into fourths

1 medium onion, chopped
(1/2 cup)

1 bag (8 ounces) baby-cut carrots

1 package (3.4 ounces) fresh
shiitake mushrooms, sliced

1 can (14 1/2 ounces) diced
tomatoes, undrained

1 can (10 1/2 ounces) condensed
beef broth

1/2 cup all-purpose flour

1 tablespoon Worcestershire sauce

1 teaspoon salt

1 teaspoon sugar

1 teaspoon dried marjoram leaves

1/4 teaspoon pepper

1 pound beef stew meat, cut into
1/2-inch pieces

*1.* Mix all ingredients except beef in 3 1/2- to 4-quart slow cooker.
Add beef.

*2.* Cover and cook on low heat setting 8 to 9 hours or until vegetables and beef are tender. Stir well before serving.

**1 Serving:**
Calories 230 (Calories from fat 65);
Fat 7g (Saturated 3g); Cholesterol 35mg;
Sodium 640mg; Carbohydrate 29g
(Dietary Fiber 3g); Protein 16g

**% Daily Value:**
Vitamin A 46%; Vitamin C 16%; Calcium 4%;
Iron 18%

**Diet Exchanges:**
1 1/2 Starch, 2 Lean Meat, 1 Vegetable

*Betty's Success Tip*   To make sure everything is done at the same time, cut the meat and vegetables into the sizes specified in the recipe.

*Ingredient Substitution*   Shiitake mushrooms add a wonderful, rich flavor to this easy beef stew, but if they aren't available you can use 2 cups sliced regular white mushrooms.

# Irish Stew

**Slow Cooker** 3 1/2- to 6-quart • **Prep Time** 15 min • **Cook Time** Low 8 to 10 hr

2 pounds lean lamb stew meat

6 medium potatoes (2 pounds),
  cut into 1/2-inch slices

3 medium onions, sliced

1 teaspoon salt

1/4 teaspoon pepper

1 teaspoon dried thyme leaves

1 can (14 1/2 ounces) beef broth

Chopped fresh parsley, if desired

*1.* Layer half each of the lamb, potatoes and onions in 3 1/2- to 6-quart slow cooker. Sprinkle with half each of the salt, pepper and thyme. Repeat layers and sprinkle with remaining seasonings. Pour broth over top.

*2.* Cover and cook on low heat setting 8 to 10 hours or until lamb and vegetables are tender.

*3.* Skim fat from stew. Sprinkle parsley over stew.

**1 Serving:**
Calories 250 (Calories from Fat 65);
Fat 7g (Saturated 2g); Cholesterol 60mg;
Sodium 590mg; Carbohydrate 27g
(Dietary Fiber 3g); Protein 23g

**% Daily Value:**
Vitamin A 0%; Vitamin C 12%; Calcium 2%;
Iron 16%

**Diet Exchanges:**
1 Starch, 2 Lean Meat, 2 Vegetable

*Serving Suggestion*   Plan to serve this stew on a Saturday or Sunday evening. Take the time to bake a loaf of Irish soda bread, using your favorite recipe. Complete the meal with tall glasses of full-bodied stout beer. This meal is so good, it will put you in the mood to dance a jig!

*Finishing Touch*   Like green peas in your Irish stew? Thaw a cup of frozen green peas, or rinse them under cold running water until separated and thawed. Stir them into the stew after you have skimmed off the fat, and let the heat of the stew warm the peas.

# Mexican Pork

**Slow Cooker** 3 1/2- to 4-quart • **Prep Time** 5 min • **Cook Time** Low 6 to 8 hr • **Finishing Cook Time** Low 5 min

1 pound pork boneless loin roast, cut into 1-inch pieces

1 jar (20 ounces) salsa

1 can (4 ounces) chopped green chilies, drained

1 can (15 ounces) black beans, rinsed and drained

1 cup shredded Monterey Jack cheese (4 ounces), if desired

*1.* Mix pork, salsa and chilies in 3 1/2- to 4-quart slow cooker.

*2.* Cover and cook on low heat setting 6 to 8 hours or until pork is tender. Stir in beans. Cover and cook on low heat setting about 5 minutes or until hot. Sprinkle with cheese.

**1 Serving:**
Calories 345 (Calories from Fat 90); Fat 10g (Saturated 3g); Cholesterol 75mg; Sodium 900mg; Carbohydrate 37g (Dietary Fiber 10g); Protein 37g

**% Daily Value:**
Vitamin A 12%; Vitamin C 48%; Calcium 14%; Iron 6%

**Diet Exchanges:**
2 Starch, 4 Very Lean Meat, 1 Vegetable, 1/2 Fat

*Ingredient Substitution*   You can vary the taste of this south-of-the-border dish by using pinto beans instead of black beans and Cheddar cheese instead of Monterey Jack cheese.

*Serving Suggestion*   Try serving the pork over hot cooked rice or tortilla chips. Top with a dollop of guacamole or sour cream.

Mexican Pork

# Italian Spaghetti Sauce

**Slow Cooker** 5-quart • **Prep Time** 15 min • **Cook Time** Low 8 to 9 hr

2 pounds bulk Italian sausage
   or ground beef

3 medium onions, chopped
   (2 1/4 cups)

2 cups sliced mushrooms

6 cloves garlic, finely chopped

2 cans (14 1/2 ounces each) diced
   tomatoes, undrained

1 can (29 ounces) tomato sauce

1 can (12 ounces) tomato paste

2 tablespoons dried basil leaves

1 tablespoon dried oregano leaves

1 tablespoon sugar

1 teaspoon salt

1/2 teaspoon pepper

1/2 teaspoon crushed red pepper

*1.* Cook sausage, onions, mushrooms and garlic in 12-inch skillet over medium heat about 10 minutes, stirring occasionally, until sausage is no longer pink; drain.

*2.* Spoon sausage mixture into 5-quart slow cooker. Stir in remaining ingredients.

*3.* Cover and cook on low heat setting 8 to 9 hours or until vegetables are tender.

**1 Serving (1/2 cup):**
Calories 125 (Calories from Fat 65);
Fat 7g (Saturated 3g); Cholesterol 20mg;
Sodium 720mg; Carbohydrate 10g
(Dietary Fiber 2g); Protein 7g

**% Daily Value:**
Vitamin A 8%; Vitamin C 14%; Calcium 4%;
Iron 8%

**Diet Exchanges:**
1 Medium-Fat Meat, 2 Vegetable

*Betty's Success Tip*   Ladle this versatile sauce into refrigerator or freezer containers. Cover and refrigerate up to 4 days or freeze up to 4 months. To thaw frozen spaghetti sauce, place container in the refrigerator about 8 hours. Use the sauce on homemade pizza or in lasagna.

*Serving Suggestion*   Here's a crowd-pleasin' sauce everyone will love. Serve with penne pasta, Caesar salad and Italian bread for an Italian-inspired meal.

Italian Spaghetti Sauce

# White Chicken Chili

**Slow Cooker** 3 1/2- to 6-quart • **Prep Time** 15 min • **Cook Time** Low 4 to 5 hr • **Finishing Cook Time** Low 15 to 20 min

6 skinless chicken thighs
(1 1/2 pounds)

1 large onion, chopped (1 cup)

2 cloves garlic, finely chopped

1 can (14 1/2 ounces) chicken broth

1 teaspoon ground cumin

1 teaspoon dried oregano leaves

1/2 teaspoon salt

1/4 teaspoon red pepper sauce

2 cans (15 to 16 ounces each)
great northern beans, rinsed
and drained

1 can (15 ounces) white shoepeg
corn, drained

3 tablespoons lime juice

2 tablespoons chopped fresh
cilantro

*1.* Remove excess fat from chicken. Mix onion, garlic, broth, cumin, oregano, salt and pepper sauce in 3 1/2- to 6-quart slow cooker. Add chicken.

*2.* Cover and cook on low heat setting 4 to 5 hours or until chicken is tender.

*3.* Remove chicken from slow cooker. Use 2 forks to remove bones and shred chicken into pieces. Discard bones; return chicken to slow cooker. Stir in beans, corn, lime juice and cilantro. Cover and cook on low heat setting 15 to 20 minutes or until beans and corn are hot.

**1 Serving:**
Calories 265 (Calories from Fat 45);
Fat 5g (Saturated 2g); Cholesterol 30mg;
Sodium 540mg; Carbohydrate 39g
(Dietary Fiber 8g); Protein 24g

**% Daily Value:**
Vitamin A 0%; Vitamin C 6%; Calcium 12%;
Iron 30%

**Diet Exchanges:**
2 1/2 Starch, 2 Very Lean Meat

*Betty's Success Tip*   Like your chili with a little kick? Increase the red pepper sauce to 1/2 teaspoon for a spicier dish.

*Ingredient Substitution*   If you can't find white shoepeg corn, you can use regular whole kernel corn.

# Hearty Steak Chili

**Slow Cooker** 3 1/2- to 4-quart • **Prep Time** 15 min • **Cook Time** Low 6 to 7 hr • **Finishing Cook Time** High 15 min

1 pound beef boneless round steak, cut into 1/2-inch pieces

1 large onion, chopped (1 cup)

2 medium stalks celery, cut into 1/2-inch pieces (1 cup)

2 cans (14 1/2 ounces each) diced tomatoes, undrained

1 can (15 ounces) tomato sauce

3 teaspoons chili powder

2 teaspoons ground cumin

1/4 teaspoon dried oregano leaves

1/4 teaspoon ground cinnamon

1 medium bell pepper, cut into 1-inch pieces (1 cup)

1 can (15 to 16 ounces) kidney beans, rinsed and drained

Shredded Cheddar cheese, if desired

*1.* Mix all ingredients except bell pepper, beans and cheese in 3 1/2- to 4-quart slow cooker.

*2.* Cover and cook on low heat setting 6 to 7 hours or until beef and vegetables are tender.

*3.* Stir in bell pepper and beans. Uncover and cook on high setting about 15 minutes or until slightly thickened. Serve with cheese.

**1 Serving:**
Calories 170 (Calories from fat 25); Fat 3g (Saturated 1g); Cholesterol 30mg; Sodium 640mg; Carbohydrate 24g (Dietary Fiber 6g); Protein 18g

**% Daily Value:**
Vitamin A 16%; Vitamin C 30%; Calcium 6%; Iron 22%

**Diet Exchanges:**
1 Starch, 1 Lean Meat, 2 Vegetable

*Ingredient Substitution*   You also can use 1 can (28 ounces) whole tomatoes instead of the diced tomatoes. Use a spoon to break up the whole tomatoes in the slow cooker.

*Finishing Touch*   Add some zip to your serving bowls by brushing the edges of the bowls with shortening or margarine. Then sprinkle with chili powder.

# Chapter 4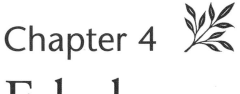
# Fabulous Meatless Meals

Photos, clockwise from top left: Tex-Mex Pinto Beans (page 76), Winter Vegetable Stew (page 72), White Beans with Sun-Dried Tomatoes (page 82), Curried Sweet Potato and Lentil Stew (page 80)

# Winter Vegetable Stew

**Slow Cooker** 4- to 5-quart • **Prep Time** 20 min • **Cook Time** Low 8 to 10 hr • **Finishing Cook Time** High 20 min

1 can (28 ounces) plum tomatoes

4 medium red potatoes, cut into
1/2-inch pieces

4 medium stalks celery, cut into
1/2-inch pieces (2 cups)

3 medium carrots, cut into
1/2-inch pieces (1 1/2 cups)

2 medium parsnips, peeled and cut
into 1/2-inch pieces

2 medium leeks, cut into
1/2-inch pieces

1 can (14 1/2 ounces) chicken broth

1/2 teaspoon dried thyme leaves

1/2 teaspoon dried rosemary leaves

1/2 teaspoon salt

3 tablespoons cornstarch

3 tablespoons cold water

*1.* Drain tomatoes, reserving liquid. Cut up tomatoes. Mix tomatoes, reserved liquid and remaining ingredients except cornstarch and water in 4- to 5-quart slow cooker.

*2.* Cover and cook on low heat setting 8 to 10 hours or until vegetables are tender.

*3.* Mix cornstarch and water; gradually stir into slow cooker until blended. Cover and cook on high heat setting about 20 minutes, stirring occasionally, until thickened.

**1 Serving:**
Calories 120 (Calories from Fat 0);
Fat 0g (Saturated 0g); Cholesterol 0mg;
Sodium 570mg; Carbohydrate 31g
(Dietary Fiber 5g); Protein 4g

**% Daily Value:**
Vitamin A 42%; Vitamin C 26%; Calcium 8%;
Iron 12%

**Diet Exchanges:**
5 Vegetable

*Ingredient Substitution*    Parsnips, root vegetables that look like creamy white carrots, have a slightly sweet flavor. If you don't have any on hand, you can use carrots instead.

*Serving Suggestion*    Sprinkle the stew with chopped fresh chives or thyme leaves or shredded Parmesan cheese. Enjoy this meatless meal with a loaf of crusty Italian bread.

Winter Vegetable Stew

# Autumn Vegetable Minestrone

**Slow Cooker** 3 1/2- to 6-quart • **Prep Time** 20 min • **Cook Time** Low 6 to 8 hr • **Finishing Cook Time** Low 15 min

2 cans (14 1/2 ounces each)
    vegetable broth

1 can (28 ounces) crushed tomatoes,
    undrained

3 medium carrots, chopped
    (1 1/2 cups)

3 small zucchini, cut into
    1/2-inch slices

1 medium yellow bell pepper,
    cut into 1/2-inch pieces

8 medium green onions, sliced
    (1/2 cup)

2 cloves garlic, finely chopped

2 cups shredded cabbage

2 teaspoons dried marjoram leaves

1 teaspoon salt

1/4 teaspoon pepper

1 cup uncooked instant rice

1/4 cup chopped fresh basil leaves

*1.* Mix all ingredients except rice and basil in 3 1/2- to 6-quart slow cooker.

*2.* Cover and cook on low heat setting 6 to 8 hours or until vegetables are tender.

*3.* Stir in rice. Cover and cook on low heat setting about 15 minutes or until rice is tender. Stir in basil.

**1 Serving:**
Calories 120 (Calories from Fat 10);
Fat 1g (Saturated 0g); Cholesterol 0mg;
Sodium 1040mg; Carbohydrate 28g
(Dietary Fiber 4g); Protein 4g

**% Daily Value:**
Vitamin A 58%; Vitamin C 56%; Calcium 8%;
Iron 12%

**Diet Exchanges:**
1 Starch, 2 Vegetable

*Ingredient Substitution* You can use either vegetable or chicken broth to prepare this great-tasting soup. If you are vegetarian, go ahead and use the vegetable broth. But if you're simply looking for a meatless soup, we prefer the richer flavor of chicken broth.

# Easy Multi-Bean Soup

**Slow Cooker** 5- to 6-quart • **Prep Time** 10 min • **Cook Time** Low 8 to 10 hr • **Finishing Cook Time** High 15 min

5 cans (14 1/2 ounces each)
  chicken or vegetable broth

1 package (20 ounces)
  15- or 16-dried bean soup mix,
  sorted and rinsed

4 medium carrots, chopped
  (2 cups)

3 medium stalks celery, chopped
  (1 1/2 cups)

1 large onion, chopped (1 cup)

2 tablespoons tomato paste

1 teaspoon salt

1 teaspoon Italian seasoning

1/2 teaspoon pepper

1 can (14 1/2 ounces) diced
  tomatoes, undrained

*1.* Mix all ingredients except tomatoes in 5- to 6-quart slow cooker.

*2.* Cover and cook on low heat setting 8 to 10 hours or until beans are tender.

*3.* Stir in tomatoes. Cover and cook on high heat setting about 15 minutes or until hot.

**1 Serving:**
Calories 170 (Calories from Fat 10);
Fat 1g (Saturated 0g); Cholesterol 0mg;
Sodium 1040mg; Carbohydrate 37g
(Dietary Fiber 9g); Protein 12g

**% Daily Value:**
Vitamin A 46%; Vitamin C 8%; Calcium 14%;
Iron 26%

**Diet Exchanges:**
2 Starch, 1 Vegetable

*Ingredient Substitution* You can also use small amounts of various leftover dried beans you may have in your cupboard. Mix them together to make 2 1/4 cups of beans, and use them instead of purchasing a package of bean soup mix.

# Tex-Mex Pinto Beans

**Slow Cooker** 3 1/2- to 6-quart • **Prep Time** 10 min • **Cook Time** High 7 to 9 hr

1 pound dried pinto beans (2 cups), sorted and rinsed

1 large onion, chopped (1 cup)

2 cloves garlic, finely chopped

6 1/2 cups water

1 tablespoon chili powder

1 1/2 teaspoons salt

1/2 teaspoon pepper

*1.* Mix all ingredients in 3 1/2- to 6-quart slow cooker.

*2.* Cover and cook on high heat setting 7 to 9 hours or until beans are tender.

**1 Serving:**
Calories 200 (Calories from Fat 10); Fat 1g (Saturated 0g); Cholesterol 0mg; Sodium 610mg; Carbohydrate 49g (Dietary Fiber 16g); Protein 15g

**% Daily Value:**
Vitamin A 4%; Vitamin C 4%; Calcium 10%; Iron 26%

**Diet Exchanges:**
2 Starch, 4 Vegetable

*Ingredient Substitution*   To make this easy recipe even easier, use 1/4 teaspoon garlic powder or 1/2 teaspoon chopped garlic from a jar to save a few minutes.

*Serving Suggestion*   Nothing complements beans like hot corn bread slathered with butter. Add a big bowl of your favorite creamy cabbage salad and tall glasses of lemonade and feel like you're on a "picnic" at your supper table.

Tex-Mex Pinto Beans

# Cuban Black Beans and Rice

**Slow Cooker** 3 1/2- to 6-quart • **Prep Time** 20 min • **Cook Time** High 6 to 8 hr

1 pound dried black beans (2 cups),
   sorted and rinsed

1 large onion, chopped (1 cup)

1 large bell pepper, chopped
   (1 1/2 cups)

5 cloves garlic, finely chopped

2 bay leaves

1 can (14 1/2 ounces) diced
   tomatoes, undrained

5 cups water

2 tablespoons olive or vegetable oil

4 teaspoons ground cumin

2 teaspoons finely chopped
   jalapeño chili

1 teaspoon salt

3 cups hot cooked rice, for serving

*1.* Mix all ingredients except rice in 3 1/2- to 6-quart slow cooker.

*2.* Cover and cook on high heat setting 6 to 8 hours or until beans are tender and most of the liquid is absorbed. Remove bay leaves.

*3.* Serve beans over rice.

*Serving Suggestion*    Try serving these black beans with poached eggs instead of rice. Place a poached egg on top of each serving of beans. Spoon your favorite salsa or drizzle hot sauce onto the egg, and top it off with a sprinkle of shredded Cheddar cheese and chopped fresh cilantro.

*Finishing Touch*    Serve bowls of chopped red onion and hard-cooked eggs to sprinkle on top for a traditional black bean and rice dish.

**1 Serving:**
Calories 385 (Calories from Fat 55);
Fat 6g (Saturated 1g); Cholesterol 0mg;
Sodium 500mg; Carbohydrate 78g
(Dietary Fiber 14g); Protein 19g

**% Daily Value:**
Vitamin A 6%; Vitamin C 32%; Calcium 18%;
Iron 38%

**Diet Exchanges:**
4 Starch, 3 Vegetable

# Savory Garbanzo Beans with Vegetables

**8 servings**

**Slow Cooker** 3 1/2- to 6-quart • **Prep Time** 15 min • **Cook Time** High 4 to 5 hr • **Finishing Cook Time** High 15 min

1 pound dried garbanzo beans
   (2 cups), sorted and rinsed

5 1/2 cups water

1 teaspoon salt

1/2 teaspoon pepper

2 tablespoons olive or vegetable oil

2 cups sliced mushrooms

1 cup shredded carrots
   (1 1/2 medium)

4 medium green onions,
   thinly sliced (1/4 cup)

2 cloves garlic, finely chopped

2 tablespoons lemon juice

1 to 2 tablespoons prepared
   horseradish

2 teaspoons mustard

*1.* Place beans, water, salt and pepper in 3 1/2- to 6-quart slow cooker.

*2.* Cover and cook on high heat setting 4 to 5 hours or until beans are tender.

*3.* Heat oil in 12-inch skillet over medium heat. Cook mushrooms, carrots, green onions and garlic in oil about 5 minutes, stirring occasionally, until vegetables are tender. Stir vegetables into beans. Stir in remaining ingredients.

*4.* Cover and cook on high heat setting 15 minutes to blend flavors.

*Betty's Success Tip*    Sautéing the vegetables in olive oil before stirring them into the cooked beans not only enhances the flavor but also helps to reduce some of the liquid from the fresh mushrooms.

*Ingredient Substitution*    A drained 8-ounce can of sliced mushrooms can be used instead of the fresh mushrooms. You can skip the sautéing in step 3 and just add the canned mushrooms, carrots, onions and garlic to the cooked beans. Stir in a tablespoon of olive oil for added flavor.

**1 Serving:**
Calories 210 (Calories from Fat 65);
Fat 7g (Saturated 1g); Cholesterol 0mg;
Sodium 330mg; Carbohydrate 36g
(Dietary Fiber 10g); Protein 11g

**% Daily Value:**
Vitamin A 24%; Vitamin C 4%; Calcium 6%;
Iron 22%

**Diet Exchanges:**
2 Starch, 1 Vegetable, 1 Fat

# Curried Sweet Potato and Lentil Stew

**Slow Cooker** 3 1/2- to 6-quart • **Prep Time** 15 min • **Cook Time** Low 5 to 6 hr • **Finishing Cook Time** High 15 min

3 cups 1-inch cubes peeled sweet potatoes

1 1/2 cups baby-cut carrots

1 small onion, finely chopped (1/4 cup)

3/4 cup dried lentils, sorted and rinsed

2 teaspoons olive or vegetable oil

1 tablespoon curry powder

1 teaspoon ground cumin

1/2 teaspoon salt

1/4 teaspoon pepper

1 teaspoon finely chopped gingerroot

1 clove garlic, finely chopped

1 can (14 1/2 ounces) vegetable or chicken broth

1 package (10 ounces) frozen green beans, thawed

1/2 cup plain fat-free yogurt

*1.* Mix sweet potatoes, carrots, onion and lentils in 3 1/2- to 6-quart slow cooker.

*2.* Heat oil in 8-inch skillet over medium heat. Add curry powder, cumin, salt, pepper, gingerroot and garlic. Cook 1 minute, stirring constantly. Stir in broth. Pour mixture into slow cooker; stir.

*3.* Cover and cook on low heat setting 5 to 6 hours or until vegetables and lentils are tender.

*4.* Turn heat setting to high; add green beans. Cover and cook about 15 minutes or until green beans are crisp-tender. Serve topped with yogurt.

**1 Serving:**
Calories 200 (Calories from Fat 20);
Fat 2g (Saturated 0g); Cholesterol 0mg;
Sodium 540mg; Carbohydrate 45g
(Dietary Fiber 10g); Protein 10g

**% Daily Value:**
Vitamin A 100%; Vitamin C 24%; Calcium 12%;
Iron 20%

**Diet Exchanges:**
2 Starch, 2 Vegetable

*Betty's Success Tip*    Try cooking the spices together before they are added to the other ingredients. This technique gives this curry its wonderful flavor.

Curried Sweet Potato and Lentil Stew

# White Beans with Sun-Dried Tomatoes

**5 servings**

**Slow Cooker** 3 1/2- to 6-quart • **Prep Time** 10 min • **Cook Time** High 4 to 5 hr

1 pound dried great northern beans (2 cups), sorted and rinsed

2 cloves garlic, crushed

6 cups water

1 1/2 teaspoons dried basil leaves

1 teaspoon salt

1/4 teaspoon pepper

3/4 cup oil-packed sun-dried tomatoes, finely chopped

1 can (2 1/4 ounces) sliced ripe olives, drained

*1.* Mix all ingredients except tomatoes and olives in 3 1/2- to 6-quart slow cooker.

*2.* Cover and cook on high heat setting 4 to 5 hours or until beans are tender.

*3.* Stir in tomatoes and olives.

**1 Serving:**
Calories 300 (Calories from Fat 35);
Fat 4g (Saturated 1g); Cholesterol 0mg;
Sodium 640mg; Carbohydrate 62g
(Dietary Fiber 16g); Protein 23g

**% Daily Value:**
Vitamin A 2%; Vitamin C 14%; Calcium 22%;
Iron 52%

**Diet Exchanges:**
3 Starch, 3 Vegetable

*Ingredient Substitution*   Sun-dried tomatoes add a robust meaty flavor and a bit of chewiness to this dish. You can add a cup of finely chopped seeded fresh tomatoes instead of the sun-dried tomatoes if you want.

*Serving Suggestion*   Serve with a large crisp tossed green salad dressed with an olive oil–balsamic vinaigrette, along with slices of French baguette. A glass of red wine makes this a perfect meal.

White Beans with Sun-Dried Tomatoes

# Bulgur Pilaf with Broccoli and Carrots

**8 servings**

Slow Cooker 3 1/2- to 6-quart • **Prep Time** 20 min • **Cook Time** Low 6 to 8 hr • **Finishing Cook Time** High 15 min

2 cups uncooked bulgur or cracked wheat

1 tablespoon margarine or butter, melted

1 teaspoon salt

4 medium carrots, shredded (2 2/3 cups)

1 large onion, chopped (1 cup)

2 cans (14 1/2 ounces each) vegetable broth

4 cups chopped fresh broccoli

1 cup shredded Colby cheese (4 ounces)

*1.* Mix all ingredients except broccoli and cheese in 3 1/2- to 6-quart slow cooker.

*2.* Cover and cook on low heat setting 6 to 8 hours or just until bulgur is tender.

*3.* Stir in broccoli. Sprinkle with cheese. Cover and cook on high heat setting about 15 minutes or until broccoli is tender and cheese is melted.

*Betty's Success Tip* Chop the broccoli stems and flowerets into about 1/2-inch pieces, so they will be tender but still a little crisp when cooked to add a pleasant crunch. Or use 4 cups of thawed frozen chopped broccoli to save some time.

*Serving Suggestion* A nice change of pace from the more common rice pilaf, this meatless bulgur entrée is sure to satisfy both young and old. Serve with a fresh citrus fruit salad of orange and grapefruit sections. Drizzle with a poppy seed fruit dressing or your favorite fruit salad dressing.

**1 Serving:**
Calories 205 (Calories from Fat 65);
Fat 7g (Saturated 3g); Cholesterol 15mg;
Sodium 880mg; Carbohydrate 35g
(Dietary Fiber 9g); Protein 10g

**% Daily Value:**
Vitamin A 64%; Vitamin C 38%; Calcium 12%;
Iron 8%

**Diet Exchanges:**
2 Starch, 1 Vegetable, 1 Fat

# Three-Grain Medley

**Slow Cooker** 3 1/2- to 6-quart • **Prep Time** 10 min • **Cook Time** Low 4 to 6 hr

2/3 cup uncooked wheat berries

1/2 cup uncooked pearl barley

1/2 cup uncooked wild rice

1/4 cup chopped fresh parsley

1/4 cup margarine or butter, melted

2 teaspoons finely shredded
   lemon peel

6 medium green onions,
   thinly sliced (6 tablespoons)

2 cloves garlic, finely chopped

2 cans (14 1/2 ounces each)
   vegetable broth

1 jar (2 ounces) diced pimientos,
   undrained

*1.* Mix all ingredients in 3 1/2- to 6-quart slow cooker.

*2.* Cover and cook on low heat setting 4 to 6 hours or until liquid is absorbed. Stir before serving.

*Betty's Success Tip*   Wheat berries, barley and wild rice merge for a tasty mix of textures in this main dish. Because all three grains take the same amount of time to cook, they all will be tender and not over-cooked. If you want to mix different grains, be sure to select those that require the same amount of cooking time. If you can't find wheat berries at your local market, check out any natural foods store.

*Serving Suggestion*   Use this scrumptious grain filling to stuff bell pepper shells. Steam cleaned bell pepper halves (any color that you are in the mood for) just until tender so that they still hold their shape. Spoon the hot cooked grain mixture into the halves, and sprinkle with shredded Parmesan cheese.

**1 Serving:**
Calories 230 (Calories from Fat 70);
Fat 8g (Saturated 0g); Cholesterol 0mg;
Sodium 710mg; Carbohydrate 40g
(Dietary Fiber 7g); Protein 6g

**% Daily Value:**
Vitamin A 24%; Vitamin C 12%; Calcium 4%;
Iron 10%

**Diet Exchanges:**
2 Starch, 2 Vegetable, 1/2 Fat

# Pizza Fondue

**Slow Cooker** 2- to 3 1/2-quart • **Prep Time** 10 min • **Cook Time** High 45 to 60 min • **Hold Time** Low up to 4 hr

1 package (16 ounces) process cheese spread loaf, cut into cubes

2 cups shredded mozzarella cheese (8 ounces)

1 jar (28 ounces) spaghetti sauce

1/2 cup dry red wine or beef broth

1 loaf Italian bread, cut into 1-inch cubes, for serving, if desired

*1.* Spray inside of 2- to 3 1/2-quart slow cooker with cooking spray.

*2.* Mix cheeses, spaghetti sauce and wine in cooker.

*3.* Cover and cook on high heat setting 45 to 60 minutes or until cheese is melted. Stir until cheese is smooth.

*4.* Scrape down side of cooker with rubber spatula to help prevent edge of fondue from scorching. Turn to low heat setting.

*5.* Serve with bread cubes and wooden picks or fondue forks for dipping. Fondue will hold up to 4 hours.

**1 Tablespoon:**
Calories 30 (Calories from Fat 20);
Fat 2g (Saturated 1g); Cholesterol 5mg;
Sodium 120mg; Carbohydrate 2g
(Dietary Fiber 0g); Protein 2g

**% Daily Value:**
Vitamin A 2%; Vitamin C 0%; Calcium 4%;
Iron 0%

**Diet Exchanges:**
1 Vegetable, 1 Fat

*Ingredient Substitution*   Varying this cheesy fondue is so easy by using your favorite spaghetti sauce, such as garden vegetable or mushroom and ripe olive.

*Serving Suggestion*   Need an easy meal your family will love? Pizza Fondue is the answer for a great weekend meatless meal. Put the fondue on hold while you and the family go to a movie or attend the kids' softball game. When you arrive home, make a quick Caesar salad using a bag of salad mix, and you are ready to eat.

# Marinara Sauce with Spaghetti

**12 servings**

**Slow Cooker** 3 1/2- to 6-quart • **Prep Time** 15 min • **Cook Time** Low 8 to 10 hr

2 cans (28 ounces each) crushed tomatoes with Italian herbs, undrained

1 can (6 ounces) tomato paste

1 large onion, chopped (1 cup)

8 cloves garlic, finely chopped

1 tablespoon olive or vegetable oil

2 teaspoons sugar

2 teaspoons dried basil leaves

1 teaspoon dried oregano leaves

1 teaspoon salt

1 teaspoon pepper

12 cups hot cooked spaghetti, for serving

Shredded Parmesan cheese, if desired

*1.* Mix all ingredients except spaghetti and cheese in 3 1/2- to 6-quart slow cooker.

*2.* Cover and cook on low heat setting 8 to 10 hours.

*3.* Serve sauce over spaghetti. Sprinkle with cheese.

*Ingredient Substitution*   The crushed tomatoes with Italian herbs add extra flavor, but you can use plain crushed tomatoes and increase the basil to 1 tablespoon and the oregano to 2 teaspoons.

*Serving Suggestion*   Make primavera sauce for your family by cutting the recipe in half and stirring in 2 cups of mixed cooked vegetables, such as broccoli, cauliflower, sliced carrots, mushrooms and peas, after step 2. Cover and cook until the vegetables are hot, which will take about 15 minutes on high. Serve over your favorite cooked pasta, and sprinkle with shredded Parmesan cheese.

**1 Serving:**
Calories 255 (Calories from Fat 20);
Fat 2g (Saturated 0g); Cholesterol 0mg;
Sodium 670mg; Carbohydrate 54g
(Dietary Fiber 4g); Protein 9g

**% Daily Value:**
Vitamin A 8%; Vitamin C 18%; Calcium 6%;
Iron 16%

**Diet Exchanges:**
3 Starch, 2 Vegetable

# Helpful Nutrition and Cooking Information

## Nutrition Guidelines

We provide nutrition information for each recipe that includes calories, fat, cholesterol, sodium, carbohydrate, fiber and protein. Individual food choices can be based on this information.

*Recommended intake for a daily diet of 2,000 calories as set by the Food and Drug Administration*

| | |
|---|---|
| Total Fat | Less than 65g |
| Saturated Fat | Less than 20g |
| Cholesterol | Less than 300mg |
| Sodium | Less than 2,400mg |
| Total Carbohydrate | 300g |
| Dietary Fiber | 25g |

## *Criteria Used for Calculating Nutrition Information*

- The first ingredient was used wherever a choice is given (such as 1/3 cup sour cream or plain yogurt).

- The first ingredient amount was used wherever a range is given (such as 3- to 3-1/2–pound cut-up broiler-fryer chicken).

- The first serving number was used wherever a range is given (such as 4 to 6 servings).

- "If desired" ingredients and recipe variations were not included (such as sprinkle with brown sugar, if desired).

- Only the amount of a marinade or frying oil that is estimated to be absorbed by the food during preparation or cooking was calculated.

## Ingredients Used in Recipe Testing and Nutrition Calculations

- Ingredients used for testing represent those that the majority of consumers use in their homes: large eggs, 2% milk, 80%-lean ground beef, canned ready-to-use chicken broth and vegetable oil spread containing not less than 65 percent fat.

- Fat-free, low-fat or low-sodium products were not used, unless otherwise indicated.

- Solid vegetable shortening (not butter, margarine, nonstick cooking sprays or vegetable oil spread as they can cause sticking problems) was used to grease pans, unless otherwise indicated.

## Equipment Used in Recipe Testing

We use equipment for testing that the majority of consumers use in their homes. If a specific piece of equipment (such as a wire whisk) is necessary for recipe success, it is listed in the recipe.

- Cookware and bakeware without nonstick coatings were used, unless otherwise indicated.

- No dark-colored, black or insulated bakeware was used.

- When a pan is specified in a recipe, a metal pan was used; a baking dish or pie plate means oven-proof glass was used.

- An electric hand mixer was used for mixing only when mixer speeds are specified in the recipe directions. When a mixer speed is not given, a spoon or fork was used.

## Cooking Terms Glossary

**Beat:** Mix ingredients vigorously with spoon, fork, wire whisk, hand beater or electric mixer until smooth and uniform.

**Boil:** Heat liquid until bubbles rise continuously and break on the surface and steam is given off. For rolling boil, the bubbles form rapidly.

**Chop:** Cut into coarse or fine irregular pieces with a knife, food chopper, blender or food processor.

**Cube:** Cut into squares 1/2 inch or larger.

**Dice:** Cut into squares smaller than 1/2 inch.

**Grate:** Cut into tiny particles using small rough holes of grater (citrus peel or chocolate).

**Grease:** Rub the inside surface of a pan with shortening, using pastry brush, piece of waxed paper or paper towel, to prevent food from sticking during baking (as for some casseroles).

**Julienne:** Cut into thin, matchlike strips, using knife or food processor (vegetables, fruits, meats).

**Mix:** Combine ingredients in any way that distributes them evenly.

**Sauté:** Cook foods in hot oil or margarine over medium-high heat with frequent tossing and turning motion.

**Shred:** Cut into long thin pieces by rubbing food across the holes of a shredder, as for cheese, or by using a knife to slice very thinly, as for cabbage.

**Simmer:** Cook in liquid just below the boiling point on top of the stove; usually after reducing heat from a boil. Bubbles will rise slowly and break just below the surface.

**Stir:** Mix ingredients until uniform consistency. Stir once in a while for stirring occasionally, often for stirring frequently and continuously for stirring constantly.

**Toss:** Tumble ingredients (such as green salad) lightly with a lifting motion, usually to coat evenly or mix with another food.

# Metric Conversion Chart

## Volume

| U.S. Units | Canadian Metric | Australian Metric |
|---|---|---|
| 1/4 teaspoon | 1 mL | 1 ml |
| 1/2 teaspoon | 2 mL | 2 ml |
| 1 teaspoon | 5 mL | 5 ml |
| 1 tablespoon | 15 mL | 20 ml |
| 1/4 cup | 50 mL | 60 ml |
| 1/3 cup | 75 mL | 80 ml |
| 1/2 cup | 125 mL | 125 ml |
| 2/3 cup | 150 mL | 170 ml |
| 3/4 cup | 175 mL | 190 ml |
| 1 cup | 250 mL | 250 ml |
| 1 quart | 1 liter | 1 liter |
| 1 1/2 quarts | 1.5 liters | 1.5 liters |
| 2 quarts | 2 liters | 2 liters |
| 2 1/2 quarts | 2.5 liters | 2.5 liters |
| 3 quarts | 3 liters | 3 liters |
| 4 quarts | 4 liters | 4 liters |

## Weight

| U.S. Units | Canadian Metric | Australian Metric |
|---|---|---|
| 1 ounce | 30 grams | 30 grams |
| 2 ounces | 55 grams | 60 grams |
| 3 ounces | 85 grams | 90 grams |
| 4 ounces (1/4 pound) | 115 grams | 125 grams |
| 8 ounces (1/2 pound) | 225 grams | 225 grams |
| 16 ounces (1 pound) | 455 grams | 500 grams |
| 1 pound | 455 grams | 1/2 kilogram |

## Measurements

| Inches | Centimeters |
|---|---|
| 1 | 2.5 |
| 2 | 5.0 |
| 3 | 7.5 |
| 4 | 10.0 |
| 5 | 12.5 |
| 6 | 15.0 |
| 7 | 17.5 |
| 8 | 20.5 |
| 9 | 23.0 |
| 10 | 25.5 |
| 11 | 28.0 |
| 12 | 30.5 |
| 13 | 33.0 |

## Temperatures

| Fahrenheit | Celsius |
|---|---|
| 32° | 0° |
| 212° | 100° |
| 250° | 120° |
| 275° | 140° |
| 300° | 150° |
| 325° | 160° |
| 350° | 180° |
| 375° | 190° |
| 400° | 200° |
| 425° | 220° |
| 450° | 230° |
| 475° | 240° |
| 500° | 260° |

**Note:** The recipes in this cookbook have not been developed or tested using metric measures. When converting recipes to metric, some variations in quality may be noted.

# Index

Numbers in *italics* refer to photographs.

# Complete your cookbook library with these *Betty Crocker* titles

Betty Crocker's A Passion for Pasta

Betty Crocker's Best Bread Machine Cookbook

Betty Crocker's Best Chicken Cookbook

Betty Crocker's Best Christmas Cookbook

Betty Crocker's Best of Baking

Betty Crocker's Best of Healthy and Hearty Cooking

Betty Crocker's Best-Loved Recipes

Betty Crocker's Bisquick® Cookbook

Betty Crocker's Bread Machine Cookbook

Betty Crocker's Cook It Quick

**Betty Crocker's Cookbook, 9th Edition** - *The* **BIG RED** *Cookbook*™

Betty Crocker's Cookbook, Bridal Edition

Betty Crocker's Cookie Book

Betty Crocker's Cooking and Coping with Cancer

Betty Crocker's Cooking Basics

Betty Crocker's Easy Slow Cooker Dinners

Betty Crocker's Eat and Lose Weight

Betty Crocker's Entertaining Basics

Betty Crocker's Flavors of Home

Betty Crocker's Good & Easy Cookbook

Betty Crocker's Great Grilling

Betty Crocker's Healthy New Choices

Betty Crocker's Indian Home Cooking

Betty Crocker's Italian Cooking

Betty Crocker's Kids Cook!

Betty Crocker's Kitchen Library

Betty Crocker's Low-Fat Low-Cholesterol Cooking Today

Betty Crocker's New Cake Decorating

Betty Crocker's New Chinese Cookbook

Betty Crocker's Picture Cook Book, Facsimile Edition

Betty Crocker's Slow Cooker Cookbook

Betty Crocker's Southwest Cooking

Betty Crocker's Vegetarian Cooking